Staniel Cay Unveiled

Travel, Taste, and Explore the Exuma Cays Bahamas

Copyright © 2024

All rights are reserved, and no part of this publication may be reproduced, distributed, or transmitted in any manner, whether through photocopying, recording, or any other electronic or mechanical methods, without the explicit prior written permission of the publisher. This restriction applies to any form or means of reproduction or distribution.

Exceptions to this rule include brief quotations that may be incorporated into critical reviews, as well as certain other noncommercial uses that are allowed by copyright law. Any such usage must adhere to the specified conditions and permissions outlined by the copyright holder.

Book Design by HMDPUBLISHING

Contents

Introduction: Discover Staniel Cay—A Gateway to a Magical Paradise....8

01. The History of Staniel Cay and the Exumas Bahamas—From Pirates to Pig Island..................12
02. Tips and Resources for Planning Your Vacation on Staniel Cay......39
03. Staniel Cay Vacation Rentals..................62
04. When is the Best Time to Visit Staniel Cay? A Guide to the Climate and Average Weather Year Round..................70
05. Things to Do to Unleash Your Adventurous Side in Staniel and the Exuma Cays..................79
06. Exploring the Staniel Cay: Event Services, Boats, Golf Carts, Water Toys, Snorkeling, and Diving Equipment on Staniel Cay....108
07. Dining Options on Staniel Cay and Other Cays Nearby..............115
08. Experience the Beauty of Nature at Exuma Land and Sea Park in the Bahamas..................127
09. Visiting Black Point on Great Guana Cay..................144
10. Create Memories to Last a Lifetime at Fowl Cay Resort in the Exuma Cays..................152
11. Little Farmers Cay—A Haven for Turtles..................156
12. Exploring Compass Cay in the Exuma Cays..................162
13. Flavors of the Bahamas: A Culinary Journey Through Authentic Bahamian Recipes..................166

- **17.** Town Beach
- **18.** Big Dogs Bar and Grill
- **19.** Staniel Cay Adventure
- **20.** Staniel Cay Vacation Rentals
- **21.** Police Department
- **22.** Blue Store
- **23.** Isles General and Isles Inn
- **24.** Swimming Pigs
- **25.** Thunderball Grotto

Discover Staniel Cay and Explore the Exuma Cays

Immerse Yourself in the Rich Culture of Staniel Cay

Have you ever dreamed of experiencing the true essence of the Bahamas? Our exclusive guide will take you on an unforgettable journey through Staniel Cay and the surrounding Exuma Cays. Crafted by someone who has spent over thirty-five years exploring these breathtaking islands, this is more than just a travel guide—it's a love letter to a place I call home.

What You'll Find Inside:

- **Authentic Recipes:**

   Savor the flavors of the Bahamas with recipes straight from the heart of Staniel Cay. From drinks and mouthwatering Bahamian dishes to delectable desserts, each recipe captures the unique taste of the islands.

- **Stunning Photography:**

   Explore the Exuma Cays through captivating photographs that showcase their incredible beauty. Every image tells a story, inviting you to experience the vibrant landscapes and crystal-clear waters.

- **Bahamian Music Referrals:**

   Feel the rhythm of the Bahamas with curated music recommendations. Discover the sounds that define the islands and enhance your cultural immersion. With songs like "Hooked Like a Fish" and "Stop the World and Let Me Off."

Why Choose Our Guide?

This isn't just another travel guide. It's a personal collection of insights and stories gathered over two decades of living in and exploring the Exuma Cays. You'll get an insider's perspective on the best places to visit, hidden gems only locals know about, and the rich history that makes these islands so unique.

This Guide is Perfect For:

- **Travel Enthusiasts:**

Whether you're planning your first trip to Staniel Cay or are a seasoned visitor, our guide offers unique experiences you won't find anywhere else.

- **Music Lovers**

  Dive into the soulful sounds of Bahamian music with recommendations that capture the islands' spirit—link to a special Bahamian Playlist by Rashaun Rolle. Visit Spotify and search for Rashaun Rolle and the playlist "Bahamian Music" Soca And Rake N scrape Music. These are songs I have loved for over 30 years.

- **Foodies**

  Discover the culinary delights of the Bahamas with authentic recipes that bring the island's flavors to your kitchen.

Experience the Exuma Cays Like Never Before

Don't miss out on this unique opportunity to explore the Exuma Cays through the eyes of someone who knows them best.

Unlock the Secrets of the Exuma Cays

Ready to discover the hidden treasures of the Exuma Cays? Experience the Exuma Cays in a way only a valid local can offer. Join us on this extraordinary adventure today!

Introduction: Discover Staniel Cay—A Gateway to a Magical Paradise

Nestled in the heart of the Exuma Cays, Staniel Cay is more than just a destination; it's a vibrant celebration of nature, culture, and the spirit of adventure. Are you ready to explore an island's hidden gems and local traditions that promise serenity and exhilaration? Staniel Cay beckons with endless possibilities for discovery, from the Thunderball Grotto's mysterious depths to the impromptu Junkanoo events with lively rhythms. For those yearning for an adventure both thrilling and serene, Staniel Cay is an idyllic destination that promises to captivate your senses and feed your wanderlust.

A Tapestry of Experiences

Imagine swimming alongside a shark's graceful contours, feeling the pulse of life under the sea, or snorkeling in Thunderball Grotto, where rays of sunlight illuminate a world brimming with color and life. These are not mere fantasies, but everyday adventures that await you in Staniel Cay. The island is a paradise for those seeking to plunge into the ocean's depths or cast their lines into the bounteous waters, offering unparalleled scuba diving and fishing experiences.

Beyond the water's surface, the Exuma Land and Sea Park is a paradise for nature lovers. Its varied ecosystems and protected wildlife make it an unrivaled locale for birdwatching and observing endemic species in their natural habitats. Rev up the adrenaline with a dive into the deep blue or float down a cut through a cay with all its twists, turns, and incredible views—it's all about the beaches, exploring, snorkeling, scuba diving excellence, and all types of sight-seeing within these bounteous waters.

Cultural Mosaics

But Staniel Cay's allure extends beyond its crystal-clear waters. The island is a crucible of Bahamian culture, where the impromptu Junkanoo events burst forth in an explosion of music and dance, encapsulating the community's joyous spirit. The artistry of local crafts offers a glimpse into the island's soul, each piece a narrative woven from the threads of tradition and innovation.

The Staniel Cay Yacht Club is the heart of this tight-knit community, where seafarers share stories and laughter over plates of delectable Bahamian-infused cuisine.

On Staniel Cay, the island celebrates its heritage with food, with each dish telling a tale of the sea and the land that cradles this little slice of paradise.

An Island's Legacy

Staniel Cay's legacy is written in the sand, whispered by the wind, and echoed in the tales of those who call it home beneath the swaying palms, around bonfires on the beach, and within the walls of historic landmarks and homesteads. It is a heritage of exploration, from the sunken wrecks and planes that dot its shores to the playful antics of the swimming pigs that captured the world's imagination. Each day on the cays is a testament to the beauty and resilience of the Bahamian spirit, inviting you to create your own stories and become part of its unfolding history.

If you're accustomed to the hustle and bustle of city life, Staniel Cay offers a refreshing change of pace. The island's laid-back atmosphere, coupled with the warm hospitality of its residents, makes it easy to relax and immerse yourself in the tranquility of island living. Don't be surprised if locals engage you in friendly conversations; in Staniel Cay, every encounter is an opportunity to make a new friend.

Sustainability and Preservation

As Staniel Cay's charm draws more visitors, preserving its natural beauty and vibrant ecosystems becomes paramount. The community's commitment to sustainable tourism practices ensures the island and the environment remain a haven for future generations, and by supporting conservation efforts, we can all contribute to the stewardship of this Bahamian jewel.

A Bit of History of Exumas

The history of the Exumas is a tale of resilience and transformation. From the cotton plantations of the loyalists to the emancipation of their slaves, the islands have witnessed the ebb and flow of fortune and adversity. Today, the legacy of those early settlers lives on in Staniel Cay, a reminder of the enduring spirit of those who shaped this enchanting archipelago. I stop in wonder every time I see an old cotton plant sprouting from days gone by.

In Staniel Cay, every footprint in the sand is a story, every wave a melody, and every sunset a promise of another day of adventure. It's a place where past and present merge, inviting you to explore, to celebrate, and to dream. Welcome to Staniel Cay, your gateway to a world of wonder. See you in paradise.

CHAPTER One

The History of Staniel Cay and the Exumas Bahamas— From Pirates to Pig Island

A Little History of Exumas

Staniel Cay is a small cay in the Exuma Cays, an archipelago in the Bahamas. This cay is famous not only for its crystal-clear waters, white sandy beaches, and abundant marine life but for the now world-famous swimming pigs, and the many movies and music videos filmed there. However, only some know that Staniel Cay has a rich history of fascinating stories and events. In this chapter, we will uncover some of the history of Staniel Cay, including its pirate past, a few famous visitors, and the beloved Pig Beach on Big Major Cay.

In the 1700s, after the historic American War of Independence, the islands became a haven for loyalists who fled to the area to seek refuge for themselves and their slaves. During this time, many plantation owners set up cotton plantations, including the Hermitage Estate. Members of the Ferguson family left the Carolinas and were the first to establish the remote village of Hermitage on Little Exuma. Also among the new settlers were the prominent Lord John Rolle and his father, Dennis Rolle, originally from England, and about 140 slaves.

Cotton plantations flourished briefly until soil exhaustion and caterpillar infestation set in. Dennis Rolle left the area, and his son, who inherited his property in 1796, generously divided the land among the slaves. In turn, they gratefully adopted his surname, and the area became known as Rolle Town. During the 1820s, it was the island's largest slave settlement. Today, over sixty percent of the native population in the Exuma Islands has the surname Rolle. We have a lot of Rolle's living on Staniel Cay 😊

Staniel Cay: A History from Loyalist Settlement to Tourist Paradise

Staniel Cay, a sun-soaked island in the Bahamas's Exuma Cays chain, boasts a captivating history of intriguing twists and turns. Here's a glimpse into its past:

Early Days (1783):

The story begins in 1783 when American loyalists, displaced by the American Revolution, settled the Exuma Cays. Staniel Cay became part of this new Bahamian community. Life revolved around fishing and subsistence farming, with the island remaining relatively unknown for over a century.

From Loyalist Settlement to Staniel Cay, Rich in Sailing Legacy

While the early days of Staniel Cay were defined by a simple life of fishing and farming, the island's destiny took an entertainment turn with sailing. From the mid-20th century onwards, Staniel Cay began transforming from a quiet, isolated community into a respected group of sailing enthusiasts.

A New Era Begins

The post-war years saw an influx of adventurous sailors discovering the turquoise waters and pristine landscapes of the Exumas. Among them were key figures that shaped Staniel Cay's future. These trailblazers brought a love for the sea, and their stories intertwined with the local community, creating a unique blend of heritage and innovation.

Building a Legacy

Integrating sailing culture into Staniel Cay's identity was not just about leisure and sport—it brought about significant development. Infrastructure improved, services expanded, and the island emerged from obscurity. The symbiotic relationship between the native inhabitants and the sailing community fostered a rich, shared legacy that continues to define Staniel Cay today.

Join us in the few pages as we explore the pivotal moments and a few personalities that anchored Staniel Cay's place in the Bahamas sailing world. Discover how this small cay in the Bahamas became a beacon for maritime adventures, redefining its identity while preserving its cultural roots.

Staniel Cay, Rich in Sailing Legacy:

For decades, the names of Staniel Cay sailors have resonated within the sailing community, and they are recognized and appreciated for their world-class prowess. A network of celebrated sailors and regatta champions emerging from the picturesque shores of Staniel Cay and Black Point in Exuma. Among these distinguished names are Rolly Gray, Kenneth Rolle, Brooks Miller, Luther Miller, Clyde Rolle, Hansel Rolle-Miller, Lundy Robinson, and Steve Smith. Their contributions have not only shaped local sailing but also left an indelible mark on the broader history of Bahamian maritime culture.

The Sailing Pioneers of Staniel Cay, Exuma

Rolly B. Gray

Rolly B. Gray was born on August 2, 1922, on this idyllic island of Staniel Cay, Exuma, to Richard and Blanch Gray. From a young age, Rolly's passion for boat racing was clear. He hand-carved his first boat, "CAMALAMI, " alongside his friends," using native wood, cotton line, and a sail fashioned from a flour bag.

Mastering the Sails and the Waters

Rolly's exceptional talent quickly saw him mastering C Class dinghy boats he meticulously built himself. By twenty-eight, Rolly married Maggie Bodie of Black Point, Exuma, and they had eight children together. At thirty-six, Rolly transitioned to the A Class racing sloops, marking his entry into the first Out Island Regatta, organized by Mr. Linton Rigg and local sailors from George Town, Exuma. In a stunning display of skill, Rolly won the inaugural A Class championship race, becoming the youngest captain to achieve this feat. His winning streak spanned an impressive eleven years.

Unmatched Victories and Achievement Awards

Rolly's many victories and achievements exemplify his sailing prowess and community involvement:

- **C Class**: Seven first-place finishes with "Sea Hound" and two first-place finishes with "Spray Hound"

- **1954**: First place with "Marie" in George Town
- **1959**: First place with "Lady Muriel" at the Regatta
- **1960, 1961, 1966**: Second place with "Lady Muriel"
- **1970-1980**: Dominated Class A with "Tida Wave" in George Town
- **1977**: First place in Class B with "Foxy Lady"
- 1980, Won Marlboro Championship of Sailors in Montague Bay, Nassau
- 1980 Ministry of Tourism's Outstanding Achievement and Community Work Award
- **1981**: Second place with "Tida Wave"
- 1982, the Staniel Cay Development Association honored him for his contributions to boat racing in the Bahamas.
- 1983, Rolly received the Member of the British Empire award from Her Majesty The Queen.

Capt. Rolly Gray & The Family Island Regatta

A beloved figure in Bahamian culture, Capt. Gray was a constant presence at the Family Island Regatta in George Town, Exuma, from its inception in 1954 until his passing on February 17, 2007, at 85. His legacy as a national hero and exceptional sailor endures.

For those eager to explore his remarkable life and contributions, you can view the **2004 documentary on Abaco Escape and Youube** featuring vintage footage of Capt Gray and the Family Island Regatta. Additionally, enjoy the **2011 HiDef musical tribute** at the end of the documentary, "This one is for Rolly," by Basil "BJ" Smith.

Capture the spirit and prowess of Capt. Rolly Gray by watching the full documentary by going to this link. https://www.abacoescape.com/AbacoVideos/RollyGray.html

This video explores the Regatta and Rolly Gray. https://www.youtube.com/watch?v=9c_4aJphM4Y

Kenneth Rolle and the Lady M

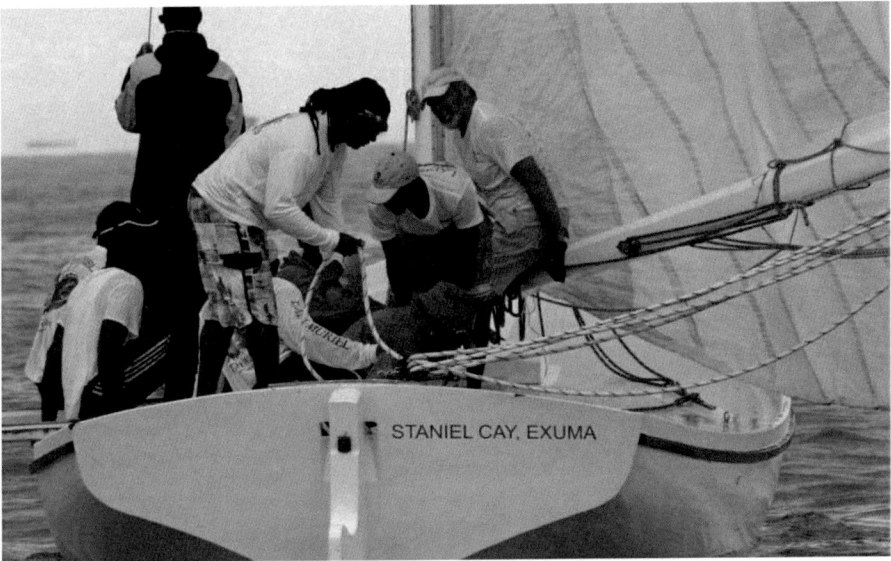

Another notable figure, Kenneth Rolle, made waves with his sloop "Lady M." Beginning in 1970 with a second-place finish, Kenneth repeated that accomplishment in 1973–75, 1993, and 1994.

The Staniel Cay Annual New Year's Day Cruising Regatta, started by Kenneth Rolle of Happy People Marina in 1975, was a highlight for visiting yachtsmen and local sailors alike. This celebrated event attracted enthusiasts cruising The Exuma Cays to test the speed of their vessels against traditional Bahamian sloops. Over its 41-year history, the Regatta became an important Bahamian tradition, bringing together locals and visitors for a unique and festive New Year's celebration.

Although the original Regatta has since retired after Kenneth Rolle's passing, the event's spirit lives on. Today, the Staniel Cay Sailing Club hosts a minor sailing event, inviting interested parties to continue the tradition and enjoy the camaraderie and excitement that made the original Regatta so beloved.

Join us and be part of a cherished Kenneth Rolle tradition that continues to unite sailing enthusiasts and celebrate Bahamian culture.

A Broader Impact on Bahamian Sailing

The legacy of Staniel Cay sailors extends beyond their achievements. They represent the rich maritime heritage of the Bahamas, a region where sailing is not just a sport but a way of life. Their stories inspire the Bahamian community, sailing enthusiasts, and history buffs alike, highlighting the importance of perseverance, craftsmanship, and community.

Brooks Miller A Living Legend in Sailing

Early Life and Exposure to Sailing

Born in July 1962 in Black Point, Brooks Miller moved to Staniel Cay as a young boy. It's here, in this seafaring community, that he interacted with the finest sailors from an early age.

A Family Tradition of Sailing Excellence

The Legacy of the Miller Family in Sailing

The Miller family has a legacy in the world of sailing that spans generations. The tale begins with Brooks Miller's father, Luther Miller, a seasoned boat captain whose expertise set the foundation for a lineage of maritime mastery. Brooks's uncle, Kendall Miller, further enriched this heritage as a respected sailboat captain, while his grandfather, Hansel Miller, showcased versatility as a sailor and a fisherman. Adding to this impressive lineage, Brooks's uncle, Rolly Gray, stood out as a distinguished boat captain and regatta champion.

From a young age, Brooks was immersed in this world of sails and sea, guided by the expert hands of his uncles, Rolly and Kenneth, who meticulously tutored him in sloop sailing. Their mentorship bore fruit when, in 1991, Brooks secured his first major victory as a captain, steering "Lady Muriel" to triumph at the All Eleuthera Regatta.

Over the next four decades, Brooks Miller would command numerous renowned sloops, including the illustrious "Lady Muriel" and "Tida Wave" in the A-Class and the formidable "Spray Hound" and "Slaughter" in the C Class. His skill and dedication led to countless championships, establishing him as an indispensable force in the sailing community.

Brooks's influence extended far beyond individual races. He became a pivotal figure in the National Family Island Regatta in George Town and Nassau's Best of the Best Regatta. His prowess was also displayed at regattas in Abaco, Eleuthera, and local meets at Staniel Cay and Black Point.

With a legacy anchored in tradition and excellence, the Miller family's impact on sailing remains profound. Brooks Miller's story is not just one of personal achievement but a testament to a familial dedication to the sea, inspiring local communities and sailing enthusiasts worldwide.

Championship Wins

National Family Island Regatta Class A Championships:
- 1999 "Lady Muriel"
- 2003 "Lady Muriel"
- 2006 "Tida Wave"
- 2008 "Tida Wave"
- 2009 "Tida Wave"
- 2011 "Tida Wave"
- 2015 "Tida Wave"
- 2017 "Tida Wave"

In 2016, Brooks Miller made A Class history at the Long Island Regatta, winning every A Class race. He claimed all the major cup races, including the Governor's Cup Race, the Prime Minister's Cup, Holly Cartwright Memorial Ocean Race, and the Hugh J. A. Cottis Memorial. A party holding and waving brooms, signifying a full sweep, filled the government dock when the sailboat arrived home! I'll never forget that beautiful day and regret not having a camera. In those days, we rarely walked around with a phone in our hand.

The evolving legacy of Staniel Cay's sailing pioneers is a testament to the enduring spirit and skill of these remarkable individuals. From Rolly B. Gray's groundbreaking achievements to Brooks Miller's continued dominance, these sailors left an indelible mark on the world of sailing. Their stories continue to inspire and motivate the local community and sailing enthusiasts around the globe.

The Staniel Cay Yacht Club (1956):

In 1956, the island's fortunes changed when Bob Chamberlain and Joe Hocher established the Staniel Cay Yacht Club. This marked a turning point, opening the island to recreational boating and tourism. With its charming bungalows, marina, and airstrip, the yacht club attracted visitors seeking serenity and natural beauty.

Stardust Over Staniel Cay—Where Reel Meets Reality in Cinematic Waters

There is a small fragment of paradise named Staniel Cay, an island where its sands whisper tales of espionage and romance under the cinematic limelight. For travel enthusiasts and adventure seekers alike, this section traverses the fascinating intersection between a geographical wonder and its brush with fame through the lens of Hollywood. Let's uncover why, after all these years, Staniel Cay continues to capture the imagination of wanderlust dreamers around the globe.

Thunderball Grotto—The Spy Who Lured Us In

The year 1965 marked a defining moment for Staniel Cay when the James Bond saga *Thunderball* captured the island's raw beauty as part of its captivating narrative. It introduced audiences worldwide to Thunderball Grotto, a fantastical underwater cave system that effortlessly matched the intrigue of the enigmatic spy himself.

Amidst its labyrinthine chambers, this subaquatic marvel breathes beneath waves teeming with vibrant marine life and mesmerizing coral formations. Even now, half a century later, snorkelers and divers flock to this locale, hoping to encounter a slice of the same excitement and glamor that Sean Connery's James Bond waded through all those years ago.

***Splash*—The Island Where Fairy Tales Surface**

The legacy of Staniel Cay's dalliance with the big screen didn't fade with the closing credits of a Bond film. In 1984, the island's clear blue bays set the scene for *Splash*, a story detailing the whimsical romance between Tom Hanks's character and a mermaid, portrayed by Daryl Hannah.

When visiting Staniel Cay, it isn't hard to imagine the calm, crystalline waters housing mythic creatures. The island reminds us that fairy tales aren't just for books or movies—they are waiting to be discovered in the hollows of nature's most exquisite creations.

An Enticing Escape for Modern-Day Explorers

The magic of Staniel Cay extends beyond what many have encapsulated on film; it offers an intoxicating escape from reality. Travelers can expect more than just historical snippets from a time when the screen glowed with tales of spies and mythical beings. It's a chance to live your own story.

Imagine waking up to the sight of waves caressing a powdery beach, visiting hidden enclaves either on foot or by boat, or basking in the warmth of the Bahamian sun with an untouched horizon stretching endlessly before you. The island's close-knit community and charming amenities—such as the Staniel Cay Yacht Club—ensure your stay is comfortable yet adventurous.

The water tinted fifty shades of blue and the allure of untouched natural beauty makes Staniel Cay a destination where reality eclipses even the most fanciful of storylines. It's a place for the uninitiated to become adventurers, for the romantics to retrace the currents of a mermaid's love, and for the solitary seeker to find solace in its quiet majesty.

You Don't Need a Film to Experience the Magic

For those picturing a serene getaway, Staniel Cay remains a compelling proposition. Whether it's the call of James Bond's once covert routes through the maritime maze or a craving to glimpse the cinematic shores where a man once befitted a mermaid's grace, the island beckons.

The enchantment of Staniel Cay lies in its ability to both remind us of the adventures we've seen unfold on the silver screen and provide a blank canvas for our own. It doesn't require lights, cameras, or action—it captivates and invites you to write your own script.

Join the illustrious ranks of those who have visited Staniel Cay; dip into the vibrant history, swim among the ellipses of storytelling, and emerge drenched in the very real enchantment of its presence. This slice of the Exumas isn't just a pit stop for Bond or a stroke in a mermaid's tale—it's a full narrative waiting to be discovered and cherished by you, the modern-day traveler.

Uncover the island's secrets, revel in the peace it offers, and find yourself amid the pages of a living, breathing fable. In Staniel Cay, every horizon promises a new chapter, and every footprint in the sand marks the beginning of a story waiting to unfold.

Calling All James Bond Enthusiasts!

Once a year, Staniel Cay celebrates an unforgettable night of glamor and excitement at the annual James Bond Party hosted by the Staniel Cay Yacht Club. Every March, we invite you to channel your favorite 007 characters and immerse yourself in a casino-style evening, all supporting a local charity.

Event Highlights

- **Dress as your favorite Bond character.** From classic suave tuxedos to iconic Bond girl gowns, come dressed to impress.
- **Casino games.** Try your luck at our themed tables, including poker, blackjack, and roulette. Will Lady Luck be on your side?
- **Live entertainment.** Enjoy live music, performances, and a few surprises that will make you feel like you're in a Bond movie.
- **Supporting a good cause.** All proceeds from the event benefit local charities, making your night of fun also a night of giving.
- **Exclusive venue.** The Staniel Cay Yacht Club offers a stunning backdrop for this sophisticated soirée, promising an evening you'll never forget.

   Visit https://stanielcay.com/event/james-bond-casino-royal-party/ for details.

A Mermaid's Cove

Allen Bauer, the workaholic transformed by love's whimsical dance, once walked these pale shores, his tracks long washed away by the caress of the ocean. It was here that Madison, the mermaid, graced the sands with her presence, leaving behind memories the islanders still speak of with a twinkle in their eyes.

Anyone venturing to explore the underwater marvel at Thunderball Grotto feels the electric connection to the past as they glide over reefs and among the myriad of marine life. Their imaginations paint scenes of Madison and Allen's undersea ballet, their fondness unfolding in a silent, beautiful world below the waves.

Echoes of the Past

The echoes of laughter and playful banter lingered in the air. *Never Say Never Again* and *Into the Blue* further sealed Staniel Cay's fate as a go-to locale for directors seeking its charming aura and natural wonders. Each project left an indelible mark on the sand-grain chronicles of the Cay.

The Heartbeat of Staniel Cay: Exploring the Island That Inspired Brett Eldredge's "Beat of the Music"

Lying amid the sprawling grandeur of the Bahamas, Staniel Cay awaits, a gem nestled within the cerulean expanse of the sea. Known for its effervescent and inviting waters, this island provides a natural rhythmic stage that set the scene for Brett Eldredge's hit song, "Beat of the Music." The music video isn't merely a collection of stunning footage; it's an homage to the island's pulse—the gentle swaying of palm trees, the harmonious chorus of the waves, and the heartfelt joviality of its people. It's a place where the cadence of the environment permeates every experience, capturing hearts and inspiring wanderlust.

A Symphony of Sights and Sounds

For those with a melody in their hearts and a yearning for adventure, Staniel Cay encapsulates the quintessential island escape. Here, you can find solitude on powdery sands or camaraderie among the joyous rhythms of island life. Waters as clear as the notes in a perfectly tuned song, beckon travelers to immerse themselves in aquatic symphonies, with coral reefs orchestrating the overtures of underwater life.

The island's beauty stretches far beyond its shores, with attractions that resonate with the soul of any traveler. The island itself is compact, only about two square miles, but the experiences within its perimeters are infinite. Explorers can venture into the depths of Thunderball Grotto and swim alongside the kaleidoscopic marine life that dances through these waters.

The Culture Behind the Beat

Staniel Cay's charm doesn't merely stem from its landscapes; the true rhythm lies within its culture. It's in the warm greetings exchanged on the paths, the stories told under star-studded skies, and the laughter shared over a Bahamian feast. The island's inhabitants don't just live—they celebrate life. They welcome visitors as family, inviting them to partake in the festivities, and encouraging them to move to the beat of the island's music.

This is the beat that fueled Brett Eldredge's chart-topper. The vibrancy of this community, imbued with a love for life, is infectious and the video for "Beat of the Music" encapsulates this spirit. It's impossible not to tap your feet, impossible not to be swayed by the rhythm of Staniel Cay.

Sail Into the Harmony

No narrative can fully capture the magic of sailing through Staniel Cay's waters, where every element seems composed by nature to create a perfect harmony. From snorkeling with the docile pigs of Pig Beach on the Big Major Cay to watching the sunset paint the sky with its palette of hues, the island offers experiences curated by the tune of tranquility and excitement.

The Bahamas boasts over seven hundred islands and cays, but there is something unequivocal about the allure of Staniel Cay. Maybe it's how the sunlight glistens off the water, or how the music from the local bar blends seamlessly with the ocean breeze. Whether you're wading through the shallow waters or simply basking in the warmth of island life, you're part of the song, part of the beat, part of the music.

A Playlist for Your Soul

To truly understand the resonance of Staniel Cay, you must feel it yourself. It's more than viewing the scenery—it's about letting the sensations wash over you, creating a playlist for your soul that thrums with the pure joy of being alive. The island isn't just a backdrop for a music video; it's a headliner, a main stage, a muse for artists and adventurers alike.

When you set foot on Staniel Cays's sandy shores, you're not just visiting a location—you're stepping into a realm where an innate melody underscores every moment. Staniel Cay is not just a destination; it's a celebration, a feeling, a rhythm that stays with you, long after the last note has faded away.

Discover Your Rhythm

Travel enthusiasts seeking a fresh beat to dance to will find that Staniel Cay offers all that and more. Book your trip, pack your bags, and get ready to discover your own rhythm on this extraordinary island. As Brett Eldredge serenades you in the backdrop of your adventures, you'll find the music never truly ends; it simply waits for you to return and play it once again.

Whether you're a fan of Eldredge's music, a devotee of tropical paradises, or someone searching for a melody to match your wanderlust, Staniel Cay is the island that sings. Come for the music, stay for the heartbeat.

The Iconic "Timber": A Look Behind Pitbull's Hit Song and Its Connection to Staniel Cay Yacht Club

Few songs have the power to transport listeners immediately to a sun-soaked oasis like Pitbull's smash hit, "Timber," featuring Kesha. But beyond its catchy hooks and foot-stomping beats lies a breathtaking destination that served as the backdrop for its iconic music video—the Staniel Cay Yacht Club in the Bahamas.

The Vibe of "Timber"

"Timber" is not just a song; it's an experience. Released in 2013, it soared to the top of the charts, becoming a global anthem that encapsulated the carefree vibe of island life. Much like Staniel Cay itself, "Timber" represents escape and enjoyment, a short respite from our daily grind to a place where the sky is bluer, the ocean clearer, and the rhythms of life that much sweeter.

Staniel Cay—A Slice of Paradise

In the Exuma Cays, Staniel Cay is an idyllic spot surrounded by the Bahama's crystal-clear waters. It's a magnet for music lovers, travel enthusiasts, and yacht club members alike—each drawn by its promise of adventure and relaxation. When the director of the "Timber" music video chose this picturesque locale, they tapped into a fantasy shared by millions: to dance the day away in an undisturbed tropical paradise.

Behind the Scenes at Staniel Cay Yacht Club

The "Timber" music video features Kesha and Pitbull against a backdrop of vibrant island festivities, showcasing the energy and soul of Staniel Cay. Its shots around the Yacht Club frame the narrative—a narrative steeped in sunshine and rhythm. The club, known for its welcoming atmosphere and luxurious amenities, became the ideal setting for Pitbull's vision of dynamic exuberance.

A Music Video Turning Point

The release of "Timber" wasn't merely about putting out another chart-topper; it signified the synergy between location and music. Through sweeping aerial shots of Staniel Cay and scenes of dancing on the docks, it introduced viewers to the Bahamian spirit—a spirit both invigorating and serene.

Staniel Cay's Lasting Impact

The song's impact and connection to Staniel Cay resonate to this day. Tourists and fans continue to flock to the yacht club, hoping to capture some of the magic they saw on their screens. For the locals and staff at Staniel Cay, "Timber" immortalized their home as a slice of heaven, a place where the party never stops and the memories last a lifetime.

Inspiring Future Artists

Pitbull's choice of Staniel Cay for a filming location for "Timber" also inspires upcoming artists. The song's success highlights the importance of choosing a venue that complements the artistry of the music. It's about creating an ecosystem where the setting, sound, and visuals merge to form a unified artistic expression.

"Timber" is a testament to the power of music and place. Combining the rhythmic prowess of Pitbull and Kesha with the natural allure of the Staniel Cay Yacht Club, the song invites us all to find our own piece of paradise, wherever possible.

Whether you're reminiscing about the first time you heard the song or are planning your visit to Staniel Cay, one thing is clear—the harmony between music, escapism, and destination has never been more clear than in the infectious beats of "Timber."

Are you ready to feel the island rhythm and explore the beauty of Staniel Cay?

A Pirate's Whisper

While Staniel Cay basked in its newfound fame, myths like those spun around *Pirates of the Caribbean* teased the imagination. Sandy Cay, just a stone's throw northward, whispered its own verse into the growing legend, woven of pirates and treasures alike.

Yet it was the catchy tunes of Pitbull and Kesha's "Timber" that brought a different treasure to the shores. The thrum of music and energy intermingled with the salty breeze as they extracted the essence of the island's spirit, immortalizing the Exumas' beach and Staniel Cay Yacht Club in a celebration of life's unguarded moments.

When Pigs Swim: The Tale of Staniel Cay's Swimming Stars

Hidden within the azure expanse of the Bahamas lies an island jewel that has unwittingly cast its swine as a troupe of unlikely celebrities. The phenomenon of swimming pigs has captivated the world, and amid this porcine pageantry stands *When Pigs Swim*, the short film documenting these aquatic adventurers and elevated Staniel Cay to a character of mythical charm. The pigs have an island all their own, Big Major, a short twenty-three-minute boat ride from Staniel Cay.

For travel enthusiasts seeking narratives beyond the well-trodden paths of tourist brochures, Big Major offers a story as rich and inviting as its waters. Here, the swimming pigs are not just a curiosity—they symbolize the island's magic, a touch of surreal beauty that reminds us that nature holds tales worth more than the sum of their parts.

When Pigs Swim has transformed Staniel Cay and Big Major from a silent backdrop to a protagonist in its own saga, and every splash and snout above water becomes a scene-stealing moment, leaving an indelible mark on the hearts of travelers the world over.

Behind the Film: *When Pigs Swim*

When Pigs Swim was more than just a documentary; it was an invitation to glimpse a world where boundaries between the wild and the whimsical blur. The film cleverly weaves local lore with heartfelt storytelling, giving audiences a peek into the daily lives of these ocean-faring hogs and the humans who live on the next island over.

Through this lens, Staniel Cay and Big Major transcend their geographic coordinates to become an emblem of wondrous narratives, a place where pigs paddle in cerulean seas, not out of necessity but as a celebration of life's peculiar poetry.

The Cinematic Debut of Staniel Cay's Swimming Pigs

The Allure of the Aquatic Hogs

A charming curiosity at first sight, the swimming pigs of Staniel Cay and Big Major Cay, also known as Pig Island, represent a delightful anomaly in the animal kingdom. These buoyant beasts dance across the tide with surprising grace and forge a bond between nature and those lucky enough to witness their aquatic ballet. This display of nature's playfulness serves as both a draw and a delightful mystery to visitors.

Staniel Cay's Rise to Fame

Beyond the Film's Frames

While *When Pigs Swim* sparked widespread fascination, it was the intertwined destinies of Staniel Cay and its swimming residents that perpetuated the island's fame. Visitors don't just stop by; they come to participate in a legend in the making, to join a story told across the currents of time and tide.

The Island as a Character

Like how authors breathe life into their characters, the tales told through videos, photos, and firsthand experiences have sculpted Staniel Cay's personality. With every new visitor, the island's legacy expands, its narrative enriched by the multitude of interpretations and encounters.

The Enduring Charm of the Swimming Pigs

A Reflection of Wonder

What the swimming pigs of Staniel Cay have taught us is that there is a craving for connection with the implausible, a yearning for tales touched by gentle surrealism. Their fame is not only a testament to their uniqueness, but also a reflection of our collective desire for narratives that defy convention and celebrate the unexpected.

The Legacy Continues

As Staniel Cay basks in its stardom, the swimming pigs continue to allure travelers from all corners of the globe. Their simple acts of paddling create ripples that reach far beyond the island's boundaries, evoking wonder and a sense of shared discovery.

Staniel Cay, alongside its swimming pigs, has etched itself into the annals of travel lore. *When Pigs Swim* was not merely a spotlight; it was the beginning of an ongoing story where every visitor is a co-author, contributing lines to an enriching and evolving saga.

In a world often dictated by routine, Staniel Cay and Big Major serve as a resplendent reminder of nature's capacity to weave enchanting tales, with the swimming pigs as its cherished narrators. For those questing after the novel and the nurturing, look no further than these shores where pigs glide through waves, and islands emerge as stars.

To experience Staniel Cay is to immerse agency in creating a legend, to dip one's toes into waters where tales come to life and pigs dare to swim. Become a part of this enchanting narrative—because when pigs swim, the story never really ends; it simply awaits its next storyteller.

Tides of Time

As the evening approaches, the warm hues of a perfect sunset bathe the island, and one can sense the historical confluence of art imitating life and life imitating art. It's as though every director has left a piece of their vision embedded in the sands, and every actor has infused the air with a touch of their crafted personas.

Staniel Cay, an urban legend brought to life, is poised in endless summers and perpetual youth, awaiting the next creative soul to discover its charms. Its story, though written by many, belongs to every gust of wind, every grain of sand, and every wayward wave that fashions and refashions this cinematic oasis for generations to come.

For those who walked the shores or dived into its depths, the island is both the canvas and the muse—a silent narrative partner to tales of romance, adventure, and dreams that dare to leap off the page and into the real world.

Discovering the Origin of Staniel Cay's Name

A small island paradise in the heart of the Exumas, Staniel Cay is a dream destination for travelers seeking pristine beaches, turquoise waters, and a laid-back Caribbean vibe, and Staniel Cay has a fascinating history behind its unique and memorable name. Let's delve into the origins of Staniel Cay's name and go down memory lane to discover the island's cultural and historical roots.

Staniel Cay is part of the Exuma chain of islands, which Spanish explorers first discovered in the fifteenth century. <u>American loyalists</u> settled the entire archipelago of <u>Exuma in 1783 and established Staniel Cay</u>. Staniel Cay also has a longstanding tradition of maritime exploration. In the eighteenth century, the island served as a stopover for British ships during the transatlantic trade and played a critical role in developing the Bahamas as a commercial hub. The island's strategic location and natural resources, including freshwater and hardwoods, attracted traders, sailors, and pirates worldwide. Staniel Cay's name reflects its unique cultural and historical roots, which stem from its early settlers, seafaring traditions, and natural beauty. The name "cay" is a Bahamian word describing low-lying islands in the Bahamas and symbolizes the fusion of Christianity and local cultures in the archipelago. Staniel Cay reflects the fusion of the British and Bahamian cultures in the archipelago.

In the early twentieth century, Staniel Cay attracted wealthy American visitors drawn to its natural beauty, warm climate, and laid-back lifestyle. The island's sandy beaches, coral reefs, and crystal-clear waters gained fame as some of the most beautiful and unspoiled in the world. Among the early visitors was the Hocher family, who built a small house on the island. Joe Hocher and Bob Chamberlain then built the Staniel Cay Yacht Club in 1956 and became a few of its most prominent residents. The Horchers were fond of the island's history and folklore, and contributed to preserving its heritage. They also enjoyed the island's famous landmarks, including the Thunderball Grotto, a natural sea cave that gained fame after being featured in the James Bond movie. Today, you will see photos of the film crew taken at the Club during filming hanging on the Yacht Club's wall.

Staniel Cay has also undergone significant changes over the years. In the 1950s, the island had under fifty permanent residents. That changed when the Staniel Cay Yacht Club was established. Today, Staniel Cay has a population of around 118 people. It is known for its luxury vacation rentals and two boutique resorts, including the Staniel Cay Yacht Club and Embrace Resorts.

Staniel Cay has become a popular destination for travelers seeking a quiet, relaxing retreat in a tropical paradise as the island features a variety of attractions and activities, including swimming with pigs, snorkeling, diving, and exploring the surrounding islands. The name Staniel Cay evokes the island's long and full history and reflects its fusion of cultures and traditions. Whether you are a history buff, a nature lover, or a beach bum, Staniel Cay has something to offer.

Over the centuries, Staniel Cay has attracted explorers, traders, pirates, and tourists, contributing to its rich heritage and folklore. Today, Staniel

Cay remains a charming and peaceful enclave in the heart of the Exumas, a tribute to its past and an invitation to its future.

Pirates, Pigs, and the Rich and Famous

Staniel Cay was once a hideout for pirates using the island's remote location to ambush passing vessels. The pirates would then plunder the ships and store their loot in hidden caves on nearby cays. Some of the most famous pirates who visited the Staniel Cay area include Blackbeard, Calico Jack, and Anne Bonny. There are rumors that treasure remains undiscovered on many of the cays, waiting to be found. There is some truth in Staniel Cay's history as a pirate hideout, but there are also some clarifications:

What's True:

- **Remote location.** Staniel Cay is in a remote archipelago, making it a potentially appealing location for pirates seeking a base of operations.
- **Pirate activity in the area.** There's historical evidence of pirate activity in the wider Bahamas region during the seventeenth- and eighteenth-centuries. Pirates used hidden coves and cays throughout the Caribbean for hiding and resupplying.
- **Folklore and legends.** Stories of Blackbeard, Calico Jack, and Anne Bonny visiting Staniel Cay are primarily rooted in local lore and legends, missing concrete historical documentation.

What's Unclear:

- **The extent of pirate activity on Staniel Cay.** While pirates likely operated in the area, it could be more evident if Staniel Cay itself was a frequent or established hideout. More historical research is needed to confirm this claim.
- **Hidden treasure.** Rumors of undiscovered pirate treasure are widespread in many coastal regions with pirate history, but finding definitive proof is extremely rare. While intriguing, treating these rumors as factual isn't recommended.

Overall:

Staniel Cay's remote location within a region historically frequented by pirates makes the claim of pirate activity plausible, but the stories about Blackbeard and hidden treasure need strong historical backing. It's best to view this information as part of the island's folklore and cultural heritage, rather than a confirmed historical fact.

If you're interested in learning more about the potential historical accuracy of specific claims about Staniel Cay's pirate connections, further research with reliable historical sources like academic papers, documented accounts, and verified archeological findings is crucial.

The history of Staniel Cay does includes many famous visitors. Over the years, the island became popular with celebrities such as Sean Connery, Jimmy Buffett, Patrick Swasey, Uma Thurman, Johnny Depp, Paris Hilton, Bill and Melinda Gates, and many more. The island's exclusivity and beauty continue to attract wealthy visitors today, with Harry Styles, Taylor Swift, Brett Eldredge, Tim McGraw, Faith Hill, Pitt Bull, and David Copperfield among the island's more recent visitors. Several of them even own their piece of paradise in the Exuma Cays. This little spit of sand in the middle of the Exuma Cays is the playground for the rich and famous and some pigs.

The World-Famous Swimming Pigs

Just north of Staniel Cay, in the beautiful waters of the Exuma Cays, lies an island of wonder home to a rather unusual breed of pigs. Big Major Cay, also known as "Pig Island," is inhabited by dozens of friendly pigs, and their fascinating stories have intrigued tourists and locals alike. Whatever the backstory is, over the years, the pigs have learned to adapt and survive on the island. They've become such a popular attraction that the world started noticing. Today, the pigs are a popular tourist attraction, and people worldwide come to feed the swimming pig.

The swimming pigs are undoubtedly the primary draw for most visitors to Big Major's Cay. When you arrive at Big Major's Cay, the pigs will swim out to greet you. They recognize the sound of boats approaching and eagerly await their visitors. As soon as you make it to the shallow waters around the island, you can jump in and start swimming with these friendly creatures. Feeding them is also a popular activity, but find a guide well-versed in interacting with them safely as they can get aggressive.

You should know that these pigs are more cared for more than most people with visits from veterinarians, shots, special grain, and baby formula.

The story of the pigs of Big Major Cay begins with a man named Wayde Nixon. In the summer of 1992, Nixon was worried about the Gulf War and how it might affect the food supplies on Staniel Cay. Since most of the food was imported from the USA, Nixon saw the potential for a food shortage on the horizon. He suggested to some of his fellow islanders that they put their money together and start a livestock farm on Big Major Cay. Few were interested, but Don Rolle, who worked for the local telephone company, saw the potential and invested.

The men pooled their money and purchased their first set of piglets, five baby pigs (four females and one male), from Wayde's father, King Nixon, in Nassau. They built a pen on Big Major Cay for the pigs and put them on the side closest to Staniel Cay for easy access to leftovers from the Staniel Cay Yacht Club. After a few weeks, the pigs became very comfortable with their surroundings and adapted to life on the island incredibly well.

They soon learned the sound of boat engines and would swim out to greet locals who came to feed them. Many yachting visitors fed the pigs, meaning the pigs didn't have to rely solely on the Staniel Cay's food scraps. The pig population grew with new births, and other locals moved their pigs to the island as they would escape their pens at Staniel Cay.

The pigs quickly became a popular tourist attraction as word spread about the friendly, swimming pigs of Big Major Cay. Then the popularity of the pigs grew so much that countless billboards, magazines, Instagram photos, TV programs, and commercials worldwide eventually featured them. The pig's photos were plastered on postcards, coffee mugs, t-shirts, and other merchandise. Hence, Pig Island has become a "must-see" destination for anyone traveling to the Exuma Cays in the Bahamas.

Today, Big Major Cay is known for its swimming pigs, and visitors worldwide come to see them in action. These swimming pigs have become so famous in the Bahamas that many businesses now provide tours to visit them. If you ever find yourself near the island's shores, grab a boat tour and come and see the one-of-a-kind pigs in action.

But what is the truth about the swimming pigs on Big Major Cay (Pig Beach) in the Exumas Cays, Bahamas? Honestly, it's a little murky. While there's no single definitive answer, here's what we know:

The Most Likely Scenario:
- We do know that locals brought them there. The most widely accepted story is that residents from nearby Staniel Cay introduced the pigs to Big Major Cay.
  - **Tourist attraction.** Some believe the pigs were deliberately moved to attract tourists, but this is not true, as Pig Beach only gained widespread fame in recent years.

Other Stories:
- **Shipwrecked survivors.** A famous tale claims the pigs swam ashore from a shipwreck, but this story lacks evidence.
- **Sailors' leftovers.** Another story suggests sailors left them, intending to return, but they have yet to do so.

The Unknowns:
- **Exact date.** No one knows when the pigs arrived on Big Major Cay.
- **Individual motivations.** The specific reasons behind the locals' actions remain unclear.

Current situation:
- **Tourism boom.** Today, the pigs are a major tourist attraction, bringing economic benefits to the area.
- **Animal welfare concerns.** Concerns exist about the pigs' welfare, including access to shade, freshwater, and appropriate food. John and Bernadette Chamberlain's family have taken responsibility for caring for the pigs. They provide healthy food and frequent veterinary services. Many locals, including the Yacht Club, help support the care of the pigs. You will see donation boxes at any store or the Staniel Cay Yacht Club.

So, while the "true story" remains somewhat shrouded in mystery, we know locals brought the pigs to Big Major Cay intentionally or unintentionally. This fascinating, if uncertain, origin story adds to the allure of these unique swimming pigs.

Staniel Cay is a hidden gem with a fascinating history. From its pirate past and famous visitors to the beloved Pig Beach, Staniel Cay has something for everyone. Whether you are looking for adventure, relaxation, or just a change of scenery, this island is worth adding to your travel bucket list. So, what are you waiting for? Book your trip to Staniel Cay today and discover this captivating island for yourself!

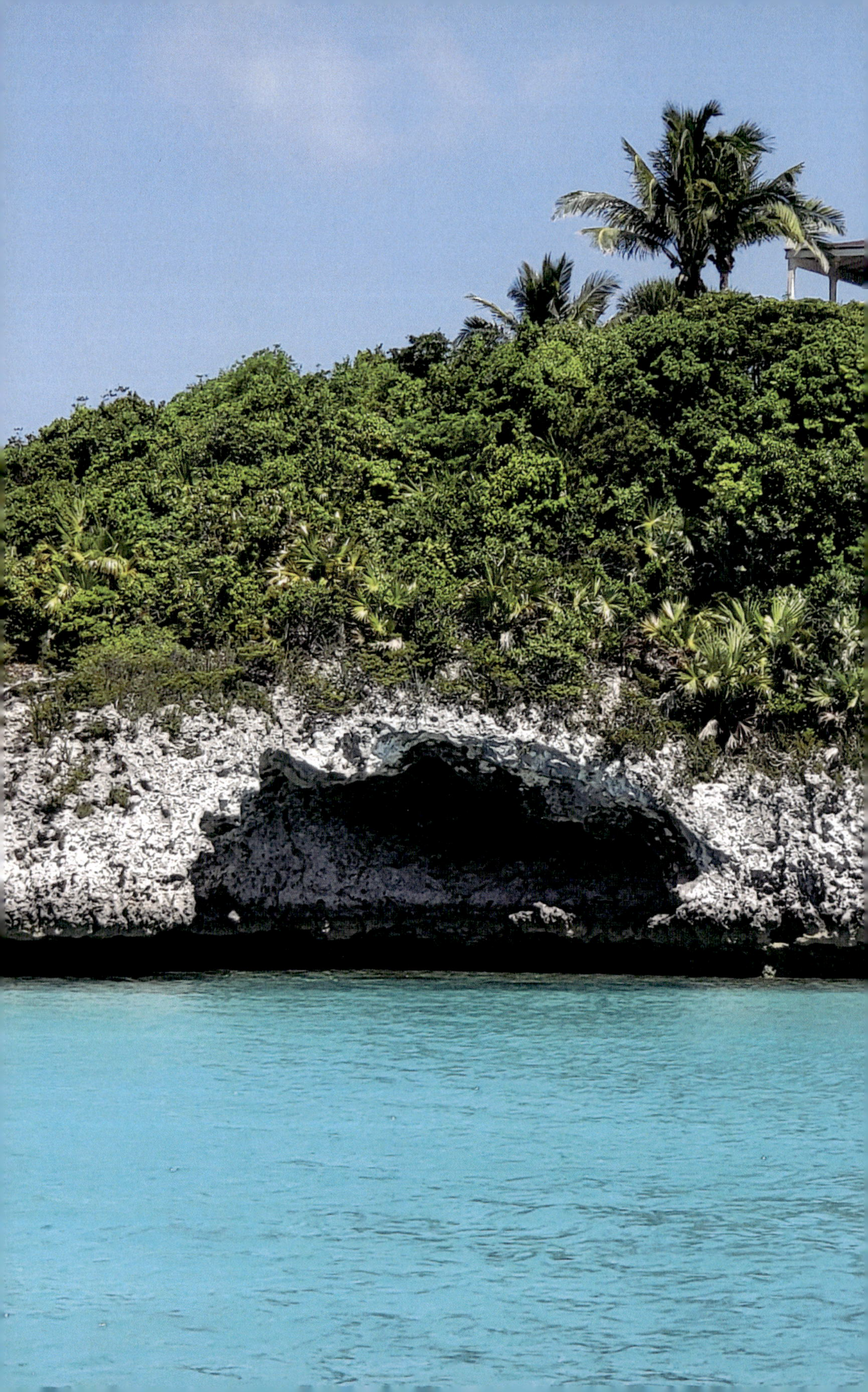

Chapter Two

Tips and Resources for Planning Your Vacation on Staniel Cay

Navigating Your Way to Staniel Cay

Beyond the horizon, where the cerulean sky kisses the shimmering azure of the sea, lies a pearl of the Bahamas—the enchanting Staniel Cay. A hidden gem within the Exuma Cays, this island is a haven for those seeking tranquility away from the clamor of crowded cities and a chance to immerse themselves in the natural marvel of tropical paradise. But Getting there can be a challenge.

Let's let our voyage begin and tread the path less taken as we unravel the secrets of journeying to Staniel Cay, a locale as mesmerizing as it is secluded.

A Community Woven by Sun and Sea

Arriving at Staniel Cay, an air of serenity that only a sanctuary like this can bestow envelops you. The warm greetings of its inhabitants—a close-knit community bound by the elements mirror the benevolent sun that smiles upon the land. Here, encounters are personal, and every face you meet is part of a tapestry interwoven with tales of the sea. So take a moment, engage in the friendly banter, and you will find stories as captivating as the island.

Embracing the Pace of Island Life

Prepare to adapt to "island time," where the minute hand dances leisurely, and every moment is savored like the sweet nectar of the blossoming frangipani. Staniel Cay tethers your heart to the simple joys—a stroll on the beach, the laughter of newfound friends, or the tender kiss of the tropical sun on your shoulders. This tranquility is Staniel Cay's heartbeat, the rhythm to which life dances, and as you immerse yourself in its ebb and flow, you find that such peace is not merely seen but also felt deeply.

The Quest for Tranquility: Finding Your Way to Paradise

Despite its remote allure, Staniel Cay is easily accessible to those intrepid hearts seeking an escape into a pristine retreat. To set foot on its silken sands, you must first navigate the journey. Whether you take to the skies or embark via the sea, there are many ways, each a unique odyssey in its own right.

By the Wings of the Wind: Flights to Staniel Cay

The quickest route to this secluded nirvana is with wings that soar over oceans—the airplane. Staniel Cay welcomes flights from Nassau, the capital of the Bahamas, where travelers can board small planes and charter flights for a scenic aerial voyage, revealing the stunning tapestry of the Exuma blues and greens below. Leaving from the States from Fort Lauderdale is also an option.

For the adventure-seeker, flights aren't just a means of transportation—they are the gateways to the splendor of the Exuma Cays. Imagine gazing out the window and seeing the islands unfold as a breathtaking mosaic of emerald and turquoise, a world seemingly untouched by time. Each flight into Staniel Cay leaves me in awe; no matter the visibility, the beauty never fades.

Astronauts from space say the waters of Exuma are the most recognizable on Earth. Now, imagine being closer to these mesmerizing waters from a plane. The archipelago, with its chunky islands and wispy, wavy lines, might look unfamiliar or even surreal to many. But from two hundred miles up in space, astronauts find it one of the most striking sights when looking down at our planet.

Take, for instance, the stunning images captured by a member of Expedition 44 aboard the International Space Station on July 19, 2015. These photos perfectly illustrate the extraordinary beauty of the Exuma Cays.

Feel the connection to this natural wonder, where every flight offers a unique perspective on the enchanting world below. For adventure-seekers and nature lovers alike, the Exuma Cays promise an experience that is nothing short of magical.

Before you pack your bags, here's a brief guide on how to reach Staniel Cay in the Exuma Cays. The airport is tiny, so large commercial Airlines cannot land in Staniel Cay.

If you're planning on traveling to Staniel Cay from the USA, you're likely looking for the best travel options to get there. This section will guide you through the best ways to travel to Staniel Cay from the United States.

The easiest and most comfortable way is to fly into Fort Lauderdale Executive Airport on Makers Air. Makers Air offers flights that take around two hours, including clearing customs in Staniel. This airline provides fantastic service, so you will be spoiled and avoid flying a "commercial carrier" again. With no lines, complimentary valet parking, and a very comfortable and modern fleet, it's easy to see why Makers Air is our favorite way to travel.

Fly to Fort Lauderdale International

One option is to make your first destination is Fort Lauderdale, a well-connected airport with direct flights from many major cities in the United States, Canada, and Europe. American Airlines, Delta, and British Airways, Jet Blue, Southwest and so on operate regular flights there.

Charter a Flight or Use Makers Air to Staniel Cay

From Fort Lauderdale, you have two main options to reach Staniel Cay:

- **Charter a private flight.** This is the most convenient and luxurious way to reach Staniel Cay. Ascend Via Makers Air offers charter services you can tailor to your schedule.
- **Scheduled flights.** Staniel Cay is also accessible via scheduled flights on Makers Air, making it easy to plan your trip. Simply transfer from Fort Lauderdale International Airport to Fort Lauderdale Executive Airport. Once you have your baggage in hand, you're less than 30 minutes from paradise.

Scheduled Flights from The USA to Staniel Cay

Makers Air offers convenient direct flights from Fort Lauderdale Executive Airport (FXE) to Staniel Cay Airport (TYM). The flight is approximately 1 hour and 15 minutes.

- Expect round-trip tickets to range from $500 to $800, depending on the season and availability.

Finally, you can take a private charter to Staniel Cay. This option gives you the most flexibility and the charter operator can tailor the trip according to your preferences. Also, this option provides the ultimate privacy and comfort, making it the most private way to travel to Staniel Cay. If you are willing to spend the extra bucks, the experience is worth it.

If you prefer a charter flight, my number one choice is Ascend Via Makers Air.

Fly to Nassau, Bahamas

Another option is to make your first destination Nassau, the capital of the Bahamas. Nassau is well-connected with direct flights from many major cities in the United States, Canada, and Europe. Airlines such as American Airlines, Delta, and British Airways operate regular flights to Nassau.

Charter a Flight to Staniel Cay

From Nassau, you have two main options to reach Staniel Cay:

- **Charter a private flight.** This is the most convenient and luxurious way to get to Staniel Cay. Companies like Island Wings and Flamingo Air offer charter services you can tailor to your schedule.
- **Scheduled flights.** Staniel Cay is also accessible via scheduled flights from Nassau. Makers Air and Flamingo Air provide regular services to the island, making it easy to plan your trip.

Flights via Nassau:

If you're flying in to Nassau, you can connect to Staniel Cay from Nassau International Airport (NAS) via Flamingo Air or Titan Air. The flight time is approximately 35 minutes.

- Round-trip ticket prices from Nassau typically start around $200.

A few airlines offer this service, including Flamingo Air and Titan for commercial flights and **Graceful Wings** Dreko Chamberlain for private air charter. The flight is just under an hour from Nassau, and the cost can vary depending on the airline and time of year. A private charter is surprisingly affordable and less stressful than making connections from USA flights. It's recommended to book your flight well in advance to ensure availability.

Airlines That Fly to Staniel Cay from Nassau, Bahamas

Inter-Island Bahamas Private Charter Flights, Graceful Wings Dreko Chamberlain 242- 359-1573

Flamingo Air Contact Information (242) 351-4963 lamingoairbah@gmail.com https://flamingoairbah.com/

Schedule as of Summer 2023

NASSAU

NASSAU TO STANIEL CAY

DEPART	ARRIVE	FREQUENCY	ROUND TRIP	ONE WAY
8:00 a.m.	8:45 a.m.	Daily	$252.00	$152.00
4:30 p.m.	5:05 p.m.	Daily	$252.00	$152.00

NASSAU TO STANIEL CAY - -EXCURSION ONLY

DEPART	ARRIVE	FREQUENCY	SAME DAY ROUND TRIP
8:00 a.m.	8:45 a.m.	Daily	$208.00
4:30 p.m.	5:05 p.m.	Daily	$208.00

NASSAU TO BLACK POINT

DEPART	ARRIVE	FREQUENCY	ROUND TRIP	ONE WAY
8:00 a.m.	8:45 a.m.	Daily	$252.00	$152.00
4:30 p.m.	5:05 p.m.	Daily	$252.00	$152.00

NASSAU TO BLACK POINT- -EXCURSION ONLY

DEPART	ARRIVE	FREQUENCY	SAME DAY ROUND TRIP
8:00 a.m.	8:45 a.m.	Daily	$208.00
4:30 p.m.	5:05 p.m.	Daily	$208.00

BLACK POINT TO NASSAU

DEPART	ARRIVE	FREQUENCY	ROUND TRIP	ONE WAY
4:50 p.m.	5:05 p.m.	Daily	$252.00	$152.00

Titan Air Contact Information 242-359-0406 or 242-361-4476

Customer Service Hours: 9 am to 5 pm, Mondays through Fridays

reservations@weflytitanair.com

Prices as of Summer 2023

Nassau to Exuma Cays flights and the destinations are Staniel Cay, Black Point, Farmers Cay, and surrounding islands with an airport—one way $125 (VAT included); Round trip $240 (VAT included). They offer two flights a day each way.

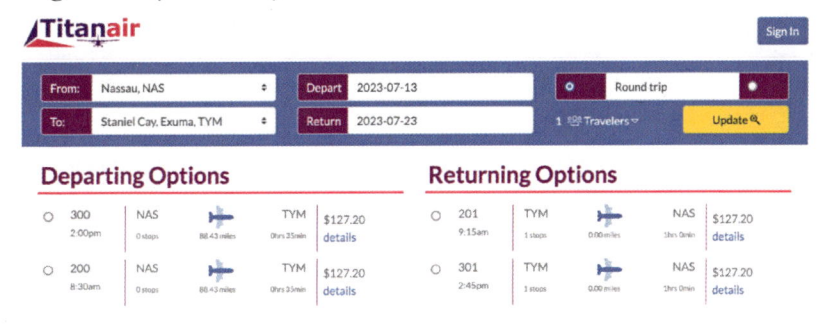

- **Customs and immigration:**
  - If you're flying internationally, you must clear customs and immigration upon arrival in Nassau. Be sure to check the Bahamas government website for current entry requirements.

- **Luggage restrictions:**
  - Remember that small aircraft have weight limitations, so pack light and check with your airline for specific baggage allowances.

- **Transfers:**

- Once you arrive at Staniel Cay Airport, you must arrange transportation to your accommodation. The Staniel Cay Yacht Club, most homeowners' caretakers, and Embrace Resort will pick you up. We do not have taxis. If you have rented a golf cart, they usually leave it for you at the airport's small parking area.

Pleasure Aircraft

If you plan to take your plane to the Exuma Cays, you can land directly at the Staniel Cay airport. Landing at Staniel Cay's airport is an adventurous way to reach the island.

Under the Customs regulations, this declaration applies only to private aircraft not carrying cargo and operated for pleasure and recreation by a pilot who is not flying for reward/payment, remuneration, or business purposes. Other aircraft must be reported on the General Declaration

Form No C7. You can complete this form online using Click2Clear's Pleasure Aircraft Module.

Sailing the Azure: Voyage by Boat

Alternatively, the sea calls to those who seek the thrill of the voyage. Journeying to Staniel Cay by boat is an experience to cherish, with the waves cradling you as you navigate to your destination, the salty breeze playfully tousling your hair.

If you're coming from Exuma, Nassau, or other nearby islands, you can take a private charter boat or jump on a tour to Staniel Cay. Many people arrive by private boats, and yacht charters are also available for hire if you want to explore the surrounding islands at your own pace and end or start in Staniel Cay.

After docking at Staniel Cay Yacht Club, many travelers have found the boat journey part of the island's charm. You can hire a boat or even join an organized tour that sets off from various locations throughout the Cays.

Private boat:

- If you're arriving by private boat, Staniel Cay Yacht Club offers a beautiful 18-slip marina and excellent anchorages with mooring buoys.
- The journey from Nassau takes about 3–4 hours, depending on your boat's speed and chosen route.
- Be sure to have good navigational charts and familiarize yourself with local regulations.

Day trips from Nassau and Georgetown:

- Several boat tour operators offer day trips to Staniel Cay from Nassau, including stops at other Exuma Cays highlights like Pig Beach and Thunderball Grotto.
- This is an excellent option if you need more time or want a more inclusive experience.

Pleasure Vessels Entering the Bahamas (Digital Submission Process)

The digital submission of pleasure vessels took effect in the Islands of the Bahamas as of February 22nd, 2021. All pleasure vessels will be entered and paid for using the Cruising Permit Module within the Click2Clear system: https://www.besw.gov.bs/TFBSEW/cusLogin/signin.cl. Bahamas Customs aims to go paperless and cashless soon, and this process is to facilitate that very same notion.

Clearing in Bound

You can watch this Click to Clear video for instructions https://www.you-tube.com/watch?v=ycehszsU25k&t=4s

- Log onto the portal using the "Cruising Permit" button on the landing page for the Official Customs Website (www.bahamascustoms.gov.bs). No username or password is required to log in.
- Select "Pleasure Vessel" from the menu below the log in fields.
- Once logged in, select "Pleasure Craft" to open the module and start in "Create Inbound" to declare your vessel arrival.
- Fill out all fields following the tabs to the right to continue the process from the Header Tab to the Summary Tab. Once completed, validate and submit your voyage.
- You can then pay for your Cruising Permit in the 'Payments Tab.'

For approvals on cruising permits, you must visit the designated customs port, and a customs officer must stamp and sign the document for it to be legalized. Approvals can only happen after payment.

Payment: https://www.youtube.com/watch?v=7gOPNEehpV4&t=54s

Fishing Permit:

The Fishing Permit is only attainable after a Customs Officer has approved the vessel upon arrival. This does not have to be stamped and signed by a Customs Officer because it is only receivable after the voyage is approved and the Cruising Permit number is shown on the Fishing Permit.

Firearms and Ammunition

Regulations associated with Pleasure Vessels carrying firearms and ammunition are:

- A maximum of three firearms, inclusive of handguns, rifles, and shotguns, which such caliber of firearms shall not exceed three hundred & eight calibers, is allowed with two hundred and fifty (250) accompanying rounds of ammunition per firearm.
- All Automatic weapons are prohibited.
- Open center console vessels are NOT allowed to carry firearms. If firearms are found on vessels deemed unfit by the Customs Department, they will be detained at the Local Police Station until departure out of the Country.
- All firearms are to remain on board said vessel.
- It is illegal to take firearms off vessels without the necessary permits and duty payment.
- The Master of all Pleasure Vessels is to ensure firearms on board are declared, along with correct serial numbers and ammunition.

Failure to do so can result in forfeiture, fines, and, in certain circumstances, imprisonment.

Cruising Permit Extension

After the twelve-month period, the Comptroller, on the application in writing, can subsequently renew the Cruising Permit for a fee of BS$500.00 each year up to two years, making a period of stay in the Bahamas three years in total. At the end of the three-year period, the vessel must leave the Bahamas or be duty paid.

A Fishing License must be purchased. Department of Marine Resources:

Please note the fees according to the Law:

[Fisheries Resources (Jurisdiction and Conservation)](#)

Pleasure Vessels arriving not under their own power for temporary importation

By Land and Sea

If you're feeling adventurous, you can combine flying and boating to reach Staniel Cay. First, take a flight to Nassau. Then, you can take an excursion/tour boat to Staniel Cay. This option may be more expensive, but it allows you to see more of the Exuma Cays and enjoy the journey as much as the destination.

Helpful Tips:

Pack light, as most modes of transportation have weight restrictions.

Bring cash, as credit cards may not be accepted on the island.

Make reservations in advance, especially during peak season (December–April).

Check the weather forecast before traveling, as sea conditions can change quickly in the Exuma Cays.

Respect the culture and environment of Staniel Cay. It's a small island with a close-knit community, so being a responsible and respectful visitor is important.

Your Gateway to Wonder

To explore Staniel Cay is to embark on a journey inward as much as outward. Whether by plane or by sea, the path to this slice of heaven is one of discovery—one that promises to reward those who seek its idyllic shores with memories etched in sun, sand, and the gentle caress of the sea breeze.

As the journey unfolds, the enigmatic swimming pigs of Big Major Cay call, and the deep blues of the Thunderball Grotto beckon. But before the adventure begins, one must traverse the miles.

And so, with a map in hand and a heart yearning for the whispers of palm trees swaying in the serenade of the ocean, we chart our course to Staniel Cay. It is more than a destination; it is a passage to the very essence of paradise.

Clearing Customs and Immigration in the Bahamas

What Can I Bring?

When planning a trip to the Bahamas, one thing that travelers must consider is the customs and immigration process. Customs and immigration control are essential aspects of ensuring the safety and security of a region. It is essential to be aware of the items you can and cannot bring into the country to avoid legal, financial, or travel-related issues. In this chapter, we will discuss the customs and immigration process in the Bahamas, focusing on what items are permitted and what is prohibited.

Before traveling to the Bahamas, it is crucial to know the customs and immigration process, including what items to bring and what to leave behind. When packing for your Bahamas trip, avoiding prohibited items is essential. These items include marijuana, firearms, ammunition, animal products, and counterfeit items. You should also avoid carrying large quantities such as alcohol or tobacco. If you bring a large amount of anything, be ready to pay import duties and VAT. VAT is Value Added Tax and is currently 10%. All valid receipts for declared items are required.

When you arrive in the Bahamas, you will be required to fill out an immigration card, which will be given to you on the plane or on arrival, depending on your travel method. You will also need to have a passport with at least three months of validity remaining before its expiration date and a return ticket on commercial flights. You must declare all goods you bring into the country, including cash, gifts, and any items that you've purchased. It is essential to declare all items as failure to do so can result in confiscation, fines, and possibly an arrest. As of June 12th, 2023, Bahamas Customs will require digital submission of their forms for residents and tourists through an app called Exempt. This new process is designed to streamline travelers' entry process and help them reach their final destination faster. Let's look at how the Exempt app works, the benefits of going digital, and how you can get started with the app.

Going Digital: Streamlined Customs Process for Travelers to the Bahamas

What is Exempt?

Exempt is an app that enables travelers to complete the Bahamas Customs C17 Declaration Form electronically before they land in the Bahamas. The app is available for both iOS and Android and can be downloaded from the App Store or Google Play Store. You'll receive a QR code and confirmation number once you sign up and submit your travel documents. These will serve as your proof of submission when you arrive at customs. https://exempt.gov.bs/

What Can I bring to Staniel Cay?

When it comes to food items, travelers coming to the Bahamas are allowed to bring in 10 pounds of fruits and vegetables, three gallons of juice, and ten pounds of seafood. However, meat, poultry, and seafood are only allowed if they have been canned, cooked, cured, or frozen. Fresh eggs are not permitted into the country, but powdered eggs are allowed. It is crucial to note that food items that are brought into the country must be for personal consumption and not for sale.

*Alcohol is allowed in the Bahamas, but visitors must be 18 or older to bring in any alcoholic beverage. Travelers can bring 1 liter of spirits, wine, or champagne duty-free into the Bahamas. It is illegal to drink alcohol in public places, and it should be consumed only in designated areas or hotel premises. *https://www.bahamascustoms.gov.bs/visitor-info/arriving/

DUTY-FREE ALLOWANCES FOR ALL TRAVELLERS

1. Alcoholic Beverages not exceeding one quart of spirits and one quart of wine (Adults only),
2. Tobacco not exceeding one pound in weight or 200 cigarettes or 50 cigars (Adults Only).

Prohibited Goods

1. Meat, provisions, fruits and vegetables, and any articles intended for human food, which are ***unfit for human consumption***.
2. Indecent or obscene prints, paintings, photographs, books, cards, lithographic or other engravings, or any other indecent or obscene article.
3. Underwater gun is any manufacturer or device other than the device known as a Hawaiian Sling whereby a missile may be discharged underwater.
4. Any article which bears a design in the imitation of any currency or bank note or coin in current use in The Bahamas or elsewhere.
5. Copies of works in respect of which the owner has given notice to the Comptroller under Section 22 of The Copyright Act.

Restricted Goods

Restricted goods are defined as follows:

- Goods imported for the purpose of any business (within the meaning given thereto by Section 2 of the Business License Act) unless the importer of the goods produces for inspection by the Comptroller, a current Business License issued under the provisions of The Business License Act.
- All goods, the importation of which is restricted under the provisions of any law for the time being in force in The Bahamas.
- Firecrackers and impact flash facilities save those, which in the opinion of the Comptroller are not dangerous.
- Firearms, fireworks, unless special authorization by the Commissioner of Police.
- Trailers, being trailer caravans for use as living quarters, offices, workshops, or similar purposes, unless specifically authorized by the Minister.
- Mechanical games and devices set in operation wholly and partly by the insertion.

Traveling with your Pet to Staniel Cay, The Bahamas

Are you planning a vacation to Staniel Cay, The Bahamas? It's the perfect place for a dream vacation – crystal clear blue waters, white sand beaches, and a tropical paradise. But are you hesitant to leave your furry friend behind? Fear not. You can bring your pet along to Staniel Cay and enjoy the vacation of your dreams together. In this blog post, I will walk you through everything you need to know about traveling with your pet to Staniel Cay, The Bahamas.

Official requirements

The first step in your planning process is to ensure that your vacation rental on Staniel Cay will accept your pet. Pets are welcome on the island, but there are certain criteria that need to be met. Your pet must have a valid health certificate and vaccination record issued by a licensed veterinarian, showing that they are in good health and have received all the required vaccinations, including rabies. The certificate also needs to be issued within 24 hours prior to travel. Check with Bahamas Immigration to confirm all official regulations and requirements.

he Bahamas restricts the importation of certain dog breeds – even temporarily by visitors whether arriving by commercial airline, private boat, private airplane or any other method.

The following dog breeds are restricted/banned from importation into The Bahamas:

- Pit Bull
- Presa Canario
- Cane Corso
- American Bully
- Staffordshire Terrier
- Dogo Argentino

Any mixed breed dogs that are mixed with these breeds are also restricted, so a pit bull mix is also restricted from importation.

The following cat breeds and their mixes are restricted as well:

- Savannah Cat
- Bengal Cat
- Chausie

Below are the instructions for applying for a permit via the government. I have completed these steps, and I can tell you that I now use the Permit service. I use <u>Get Your Bahamas Pet Import Permit Online</u>

He is GREAT! https://www.bahamaspetpermit.com/ *Open 9 am and 7 pm Bahamas (GMT -5) time.*

email: bahamaspetpermit@gmail.com
call or text:
+1-242-544-1698 (Bahamas) Also on WhatsApp
+1-954-213-7832 (USA)

An import permit is required to import dogs and cats, and must accompany the animal at the time of import. All conditions listed on the permit must be satisfied or the animal may be refused entry or confiscated and disposed of as a disease risk. Currently, the application processing fee for a dog or cat is for **US $10.00 plus 12% VAT bringing the total cost to $11.20.** A veterinary health certificate is required at the time of import which should include certification that the animal is healthy, has an active immunity against rabies and satisfies all other health requirements.

Dog Permit

A dog permit allows persons to import and export dogs.

Eligibility

There are no eligibility criteria for this service.

Process

1. Applicant completes and submits Application to Import Domestic Animal Form.
2. Applicant pays the relevant fees.
3. After approval, the applicant is issued with the Dog Permit.
4. The applicant will be given a Veterinarian Form (AGR/VS/1A Form) which must be completed by a registered Veterinarian 24 hours prior to travel.
5. Applicant submits the Dog Permit and Completed Veterinarian Form to an Agricultural Officer and Customs Officer at the port of entry or departure.

This service can be accessed at the following location:

Department of Agriculture
Darville's Business Complex
Gladstone and Munnings Roads
P.O. Box N3028
Nassau, New Providence
The Bahamas
Tel. (242) 397-7450/325-7438
Fax. (242) 325-3960
E-mail: minagriculturemarine@bahamas.gov.bs
Opening hours: 9:00 am to 5:00 pm, Monday to Friday, except public holidays

Application Form can be downloaded from his website

- Application to Import Domestic Animal (Dog) into the Bahamas.

Choosing Your Mode of Transportation

When planning to travel with your pet, it is essential to consider the mode of transportation. You can take your pet with you on a private boat or yacht, and there are also several airlines that allow pets to travel as passengers on board. Some airlines require pets to travel in the cargo hold, while others allow smaller pets in the cabin. You just need to ensure that you follow the airline's pet travel guidelines and, of course, check with your vet on what travel options would work best for your pet.

Providing Basic Needs

When you travel with your pet, it's essential to make sure that they have all the basic needs. Carrying their food and water is a must, as well as their litter box or poop baggies. Your pet will need a comfortable place to sleep

– consider packing their favorite bed or a blanket that they could snuggle with. Don't forget to bring favorite toys or distractions for them as well, this will help them feel more comfortable in unfamiliar surroundings.

What to do on Staniel Cay with Your Pet

Staniel Cay has a variety of activities that you and your pet can enjoy together. Take long walks on the white sand beaches or swim in crystal clear blue waters. Rent a boat or take a boat tour to explore nearby islands, and don't forget to take your pup to the top of Boo Boo Hill to enjoy the breathtaking views. Staniel Cay also has a pet-friendly resort, where you can stay and enjoy amenities such as swimming pools, restaurants, and private beaches.

Safety and Precautions

Traveling with your pet to Staniel Cay requires a few extra precautions. Sandy beaches can cause sand impaction if your pet ingests too much sand, which can lead to intestinal obstructions. Make sure to keep a close eye on your pet and restrict their exposure to sand ingestion. Protecting your pet from sunburn is also a must; their skin can be sensitive to UV rays, and they can get sunburned easily. If your pet has a history of getting car sick, talk to your vet ahead of time and plan accordingly.

Traveling with your pet to Staniel Cay, The Bahamas, is a fun and exciting experience. It's important to research and plan ahead to ensure a smooth and safe vacation for both you and your pet. Take the time to make sure you have all the necessary documentation and basic needs for your pet while also ensuring their safety is the top priority. With proper preparations, your pet can fully enjoy the adventure with you on this island paradise.

A Guide to Money, Banks, Cash, and Credit Cards for Travelers

If you plan to visit the Bahamas, familiarize yourself with the local currency, banks, cash, and credit cards. Being a popular tourist destination, the Bahamas attracts many arrivals each year. However, the monetary system in the Bahamas may differ from your home country, and navigating the financial landscape can be tricky. To help you have a hassle-free experience in the Bahamas, we've compiled a guide that covers everything you need to know about money and banking in the Bahamas.

Currency

The Bahamian Dollar (BSD) is the official currency of the Bahamas, and it holds an equal value to the US Dollar. Stores, restaurants, and hotels widely accept both currencies and you can use them interchangeably. It's important to note that some vendors may give you change in Bahamian Dollars, especially if your purchase is below $20.

Cash

Cash is a widely accepted payment method in the Bahamas; vendors typically prefer it. It's a good idea to carry cash with you, especially when shopping in local or small markets and stores. ATMs are **not available on Staniel Cay or in any of the Exuma Cays**.

Credit Cards

Most shops, restaurants, and hotels in the Bahamas accept credit cards—although the smaller ones do not—so you can carry your card for convenience. However, it's essential to note that some establishments may only accept a particular credit card, and it's wise to carry a VISA or Master card, as they are widely accepted. Only a few small businesses accept an AMEX card. Be sure to inform your bank about your upcoming trip to the Bahamas so they don't flag your card for suspected fraud. It's also advisable to check the exchange rate and international transaction fees before using your credit card.

Note: Most businesses in the Bahamas charge an added 5% credit card processing fee on top of your purchase, which is the fee the bank charges them. Cash is king, so to speak.

Banks

If you need to exchange money, it's advised to do it at the bank or authorized exchange centers prior to arrival. You will not find this service in Exuma Cays as there is no bank or ATM.

Travelers Cheques

Traveler's cheques are gradually becoming obsolete due to the convenience of credit and debit cards. I highly recommend avoiding them.

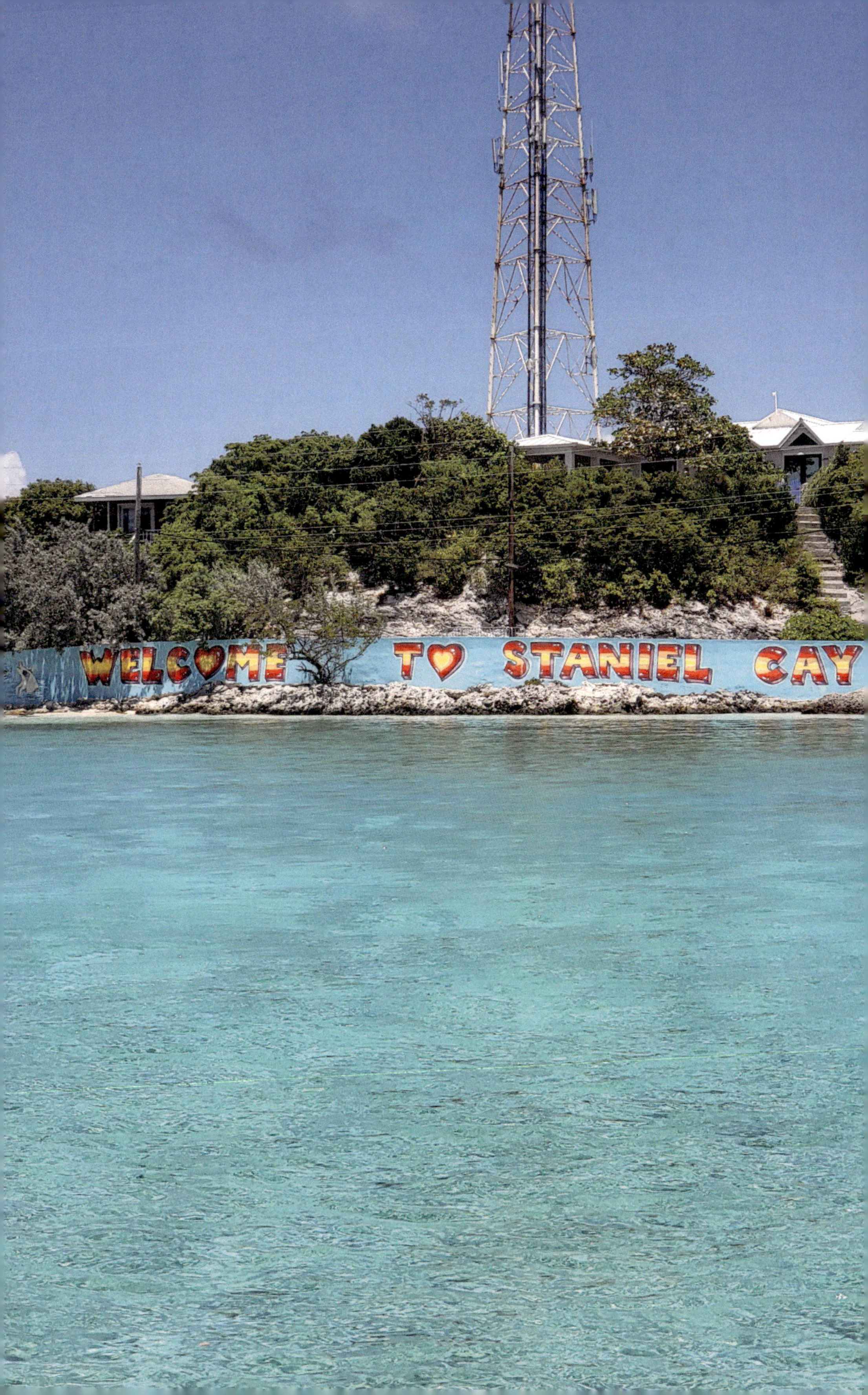
WELCOME TO STANIEL CAY

Chapter Three

Staniel Cay Vacation Rentals

Finding the Perfect Vacation Rental on Beautiful and Historic Staniel Cay, Bahamas

Introduction

Welcome to the tropical paradise of Staniel Cay, Bahamas! Whether you're a travel enthusiast, vacation planner, or beach lover, Staniel Cay offers an array of stunning vacation rentals that promise an unforgettable Bahamian escape. This chapter comprehensively guides some of the island's most exquisite accommodations. From cozy cottages to luxurious beachfront villas, we've curated a list of the best places to stay on Staniel Cay. If you know of any rental gems we might have missed, please share them with us.

Honeycomb Cottage

Capacity: 3 guests

Bedrooms: 1

Bathrooms: 1

Nestled in a picturesque setting, Honeycomb Cottage is perfect for a small group or a romantic getaway. With its charming interiors and close proximity to the beach, this cottage offers a cozy retreat. View on Airbnb

Cozy Cottage

Capacity: 2 guests

Despite the listing on Airbnb stating Black Point, Cozy Cottage is actually located on Staniel Cay. This intimate retreat is ideal for couples looking to enjoy the island's serene beauty.

View on Airbnb

Sweet Cottage Studio on Staniel Cay

Capacity: 2 guests

Bedrooms: Studio

Bathrooms: 1

Located right on the beach, Sweet Cottage Studio is a new addition to Staniel Cay's vacation rentals, completed in 2020. The studio offers breathtaking ocean views, a fully equipped kitchen, and a private dock space.

View on Airbnb

Temptress

Capacity: 10 guests

Bedrooms: 5

Bathrooms: 5

Temptress is a luxurious oceanfront beach house with two beautifully furnished levels that can be rented together or separately. The upper level boasts three bedrooms, three baths, a high-end kitchen, and a living room with a deck overlooking the water. The lower level features two bedrooms, two baths, a full kitchen, and a living room with another deck offering stunning water views.

https://stanielcayrentals.com/

Gibraltar

Capacity: 8 guests

Bedrooms: 4

Gibraltar is a recently renovated beachfront vacation home offering exceptional views, comfort, privacy, and relaxation. It serves as the perfect base to explore all that Staniel Cay has to offer.

https://www.gibraltarstanielcay.com/

On The Rocks

Capacity: 3 guests

Bedrooms: 1

One Bedroom Apartment Plus Private Outside Shower and HUGE Patio

Imagine a vacation rental that feels like a home away from home, equipped with all the luxuries you would never expect in a typical rental. Our one-bedroom retreat on Staniel Cay is designed to offer an unparalleled vacation experience, ensuring every detail caters to your comfort and pleasure.

https://vacationrentalsstanielcay.com/

Palm Top Villas

Situated on the northern end of Staniel Cay, Palm Top Villas are the epitome of luxury and seclusion. These villas offer private powdery white sandy beaches, inlet lagoons, and unforgettable views. When the tide is low, walk across to a deserted island and picnic with the stingrays and turtles.

https://www.palmtopvillas.com/

Yacht Charters & House Rentals

Staniel Cay Yacht Club offers a tremendous blend of yacht charters and vacation rentals in addition to their bungalows and villas. Experience the ultimate Bahamian adventure with their luxurious accommodations and tailored itineraries.

https://stanielcay.com/rentals-charters/

Ruby

Capacity: 5 guests

Bedrooms: 2

Bathrooms: 2

View Listing on Airbnb

Ruby offers modern amenities and beautiful ocean views, making it an excellent choice for families or small groups.

Swept Away

Capacity: 6 guests

Bedrooms: 2

Bathrooms: 2

The Most Humble Abode provides a comfortable stay with its furnished interiors and serene surroundings.

View Listing on Airbnb

The Good Life

Capacity: 4 guests

Bedrooms: 2

Bathrooms: 2

View Listing on Airbnb

The Good Life is a private elevated villa with stunning ocean views and modern amenities, **perfect for those seeking a tranquil escape.**

Tides Edge

Capacity: 2 guests

Bedrooms: 1

Bathrooms: 1 with additional private outdoor shower

Imagine a vacation rental that feels like a home away from home, equipped with all the luxuries you would never expect in a typical rental. This one-bedroom retreat on Staniel Cay is designed to offer an unparalleled vacation experience, ensuring every detail caters to your comfort and pleasure. From Yeti coolers and beach toys to the prefect location this apartment is the place to call home while on vacation.

https://vacationrentalsstanielcay.com/

Isles Inn:

Isles Inn Bahamas is located above Isles General Store in the creek across from the village. Offering several one-bedroom apartments.

> https://www.islesinnbahamas.com/

Secluded Beach Cottage

> **Capacity:** 4 guests
>
> **Bedrooms:** 2
>
> **Bathrooms:** 2
>
> View Listing on Airbnb

This ocean-view cottage offers a secluded retreat with easy access to the beach. It's an ideal spot for those looking to unwind and enjoy the natural beauty of Staniel Cay.

Lazy Bay Villas:

> Three villas offering modern amenities and staffed services.
>
> https://stanielrental.com/

Staniel Cay Yacht Club:

The world famous Staniel Cay Yacht Club offers a variety of waterfront cottages, bungalows and villas, and yacht charters. Sip an island cocktail and watch the gorgeous Bahamian sunsets from your private porch while nurse sharks and rays glide through the waters below you. They offer small boats with your rental and all-inclusive packages. The SCYC is one of those places you'll never want to leave.

Staniel Cay Yacht Club https://stanielcay.com

Chamberlain's Cottage Rentals:

Family-friendly cottages with easy accessibility to Staniel Cay's attractions. They have eight cottages and a two-bedroom house for rent. Each cottage with there own unique style painted by local artist Bernadette Chamberlain.

https://www.stanielcaychamberlaincottages.com/

Serenity Cottage and Dock House: Serenity Cottage is a private two-bedroom, one-bath waterfront cottage on the tiny island of Staniel Cay, Exumas, Bahamas overlooking Thunderball Grotto

Serenity Dock House

The Dock-House is spacious and efficient, with a king bed, bath, small kitchen, and spacious deck overlooking the water. WiFi and Satellite TV included. Adults only. We call it our "Honeymoon Suite".

Serenity Dock

Serenity has a 78-foot face dock with 8-feet at low water.

A total of 200 amps of electric is available: one 100 and two 50/30 amp connections.

Tie-off piling on south end is 30' from the main dock.

The dock is available to large yachts (up to 80') in combination with shore accommodations in either Serenity Cottage or Serenity Dock House, but it is also available to visiting yachts wanting more private dockage.

Layin' Low Villas ~ Sunset and Sunrise are Two Villas Offering 4 bedrooms, 2.5 baths

Perfect for large families or families traveling together

http://www.stanielrentals.com/layin-low.html

Contact Marty or Coral: 954-769-0155 or 954-304-5852

http://www.stanielrentals.com/serenity-dock-house.html

Staniel Cay offers an array of vacation rentals tailored to suit various preferences and group sizes. Whether you're seeking a cozy beachfront cottage for two or a luxurious villa for a family gathering, this island has it all.

Ready to plan your dream vacation? Visit our website and book your stay today! If you know of any rentals we've missed, please let us know—we're always looking to share the best of Staniel Cay with fellow travel enthusiasts.

Conclusion

Staniel Cay is a treasure trove of stunning vacation rentals, each offering unique experiences and unmatched beauty. Whether you're looking for a luxurious beachfront villa or a cozy cottage by the sea, this guide has something for every traveler. Ready to book your dream vacation? Explore these listings and find the perfect rental for your next island getaway.

For more personalized recommendations or to add your favorite rental to our list, please visit [Staniel Cay Rentals](#) and get in touch with us. Happy travels!

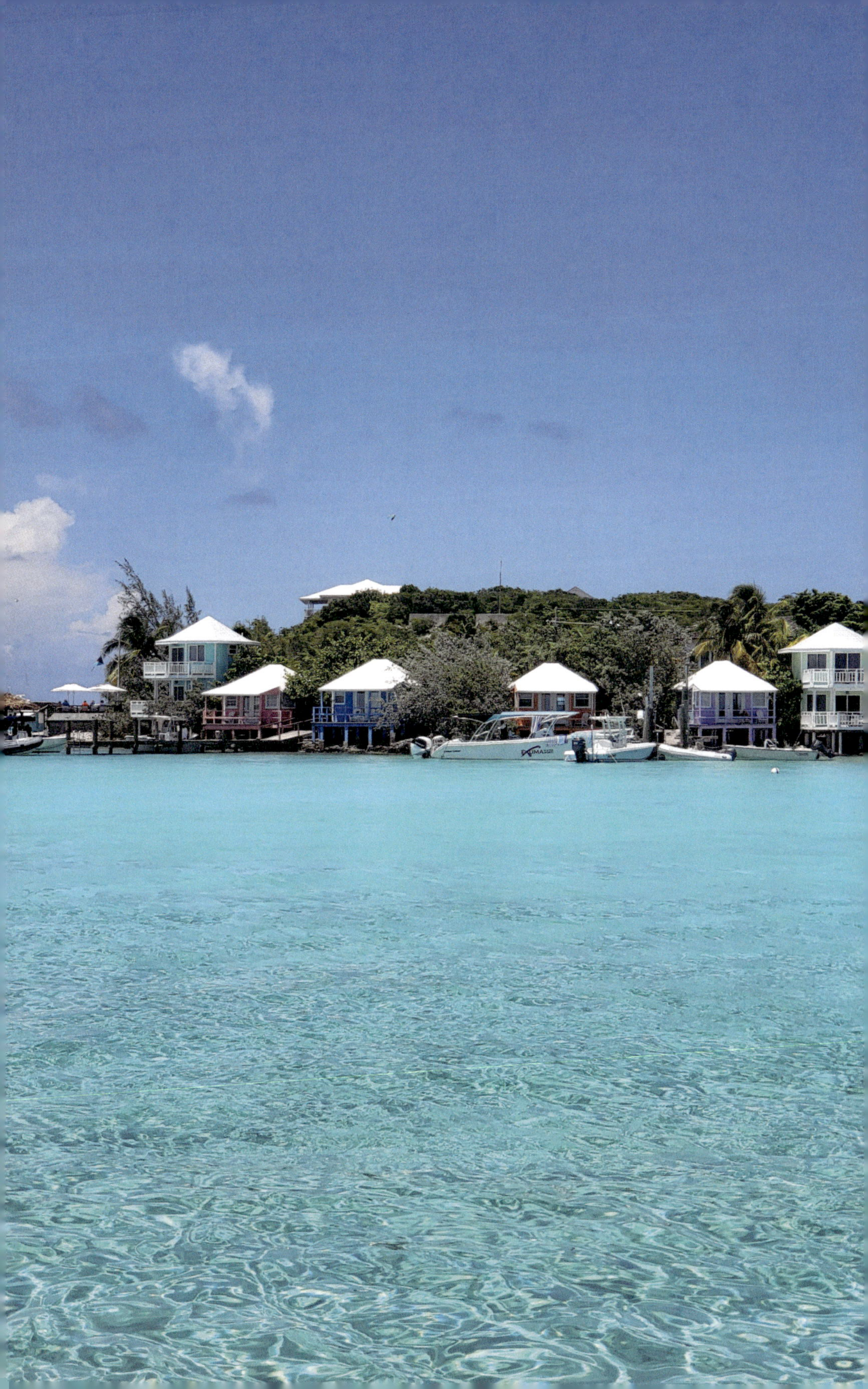

CHAPTER *Four*

When is the Best Time to Visit Staniel Cay? A Guide to the Climate and Average Weather Year Round

If you're fantasizing about a warm tropical getaway, Staniel Cay is a top choice. With its vibrant blue waters, it's no wonder this destination is on everyone's bucket list. However, it's essential to know when the best time to visit is to make the most of your vacation. Truthfully, any time of the year is the perfect time to visit. August and September have the least number of visitors, so you will find the best availability and maybe even a few deals. Let's dive into the average climate and weather of the middle Exuma Cays and reveal the best time to make your trip.

The middle Exuma Cays has a tropical climate, meaning the temperature remains high throughout the year. However, the best time to visit depends on your preferences. If you love warm weather and do not mind the crowds, the summer months from June to August might be perfect. In June and July, many families with school-age children visit, and the local children are home from their boarding schools, making the islands come to life with children's activities. You will also see lots of boaters because the water is "Flat Calm."

Experience balmy weather for four solid months, from June to October, with average highs that climb above 86°F. August is the peak of Black Point's summer heat, with temperatures simmering to an average of 88°F and not dropping lower than a comfortable 79°F.

Savor the cool breeze of the winter months that stretch for nearly four months, from December to March. Average daily highs touch no warmer than 80°F. Brace yourself for the chilliest time of the year in Black Point, when temperatures drop to an average low of 69°F in January. But with January daytime temperatures climbing to 78°F, it's still a great time to enjoy the velvet-textured winters of Black Point.

For beach and pool lovers, the best time to visit Staniel Cay and have a delightful time is mid-January to mid-May and late October to mid-January. The beaches will be less crowded, and temperatures could soar up to 80s and mid-70s, respectively. If you treasure peaceful and less inhibited moments, the latter provides the perfect opportunity to take in nature and escape the bustle of tourist activities.

If you're an adventurer and want to witness the swimming pigs, April, May, October, and November are the best times to visit. During these months, the weather can be warm and comfortable in the low to mid-80s with clear skies. Also, since it's not peak season, fewer people visit the area, leaving more time for you to take advantage of other activities.

Get Ready to Dodge the Raindrops in the Middle of Exuma Cays!

A wet day is any day with at least 0.04 inches of precipitation. I have lived on Staniel Cay for over sixteen years, and most of the year, we pray for rain as it often blows right past us. When it does rain, it comes and goes quickly, with the sun coming right back out. Keep that sunscreen on; even if we get a cloudy day, the sun will fool you with an intense sunburn. The chance of a wet day changes throughout the year, with the wetter season lasting from mid-May to the end of October. During this time, there's over a 20% chance of rain.

June has the wettest days, averaging 8.3 days with an average rainfall of 2.1 inches, while the month with the least rain is December, with an average rainfall of 0.5 inches. On the bright side, the drier season lasts from the end of October to mid-May. Rain alone is the most common form of precipitation throughout the year, peaking at a 34% chance on June 2. But don't let that rain on your parade—just over a third of those days have rain alone. Stay prepared and enjoy whatever the weather brings! There is still a lot of fun to be had. On Staniel Cay, people gather and play board games, cards, ring toss and pick up a pool cue on rainy days.

We always hear can I swim in December? I have had Decembers where I would jump in and join my friends visiting from the north, and I have had Decembers where you won't catch me in the water. The average water temperature experiences *some* seasonal variation over the year.

The time of year with warmer water lasts for nearly four months, from the end of June to mid-October, with an average temperature above 83°F. While the month with the warmest water is August, with an average temperature of *85°F*, the water is *hot* to me to swim in then. However, the time of year with cooler water lasts for four months, from the end of December to late April, with an average temperature below 78°F. The month with the most incredible water is February, with an average temperature of 76°F.

Suppose you're interested in general outdoor tourist activities such as hiking and sightseeing. In that case, the winner is the coolest months of late November to mid-April, with the second week of February being the peak time to visit. However, if you're more of a beach person, opt for mid-January to mid-May and from late October to mid-January. And, to maximize your fun under the sun, visit during the second week of April for the best beach days.

For a detailed weather summary, visit https://weatherspark.com/ and search for Black Point, the Bahamas.

Staniel Cay is a tropical destination you can visit almost all year round. However, it's critical to consider the season that works well for you to enjoy the area's excellent features. Whether you're seeking warm weather, fewer crowds, or lower prices, the best time to visit differs and can enhance your vacation experience. Use this guide to select the perfect time for you and have an unforgettable time in this paradise.

My Favorite Rainy Day Song is by Phil Stubbs "Da Frogs"

This came out in the 90s

Don't be alarmed my name is Sam and I mean no harm, He said with a blink, "please buy me a drink, my pockets out of sync".

I'll tell you a story, lets take a walk, lets talk ole talk. "Was raining one morning as I was walking I heard the froggies talk, He said

CHORUS: The frog say correct on a rainy morning (it was a rainy day), The frog say correct on a rainy morning (thats what the froggie say). Good morning good morning how are you this mornin' (thats what the froggie say) It was hopping and leaping and jumping and skipping(on a rainy day) "All summer long, we been waiting for rain", one frog explain, "Now we so happy, we gon have a party, excuse us for actin' insane." One leap from the pond start a talkin' "Mista, its plenty a we, once we was tadpoles now we dun' full grown, come back to the pond, come see." He say

CHORUS Ask them a question, they'll tell you no lie, he said with a sigh, too many times they may squirt in ya eye, oh he seem so high, he say I got to go now, I'll see you aroun', I got my load, if you need to find me to back up this story, meet me by the little dirt road.

CHORUS 1&1 (two) correct 2&2 (four) 3&3 (six) 4&4 (eight) 5&5 (ten) 6&6 (twelve) What the frog say? The frog say correct (x10)

Listen here https://www.youtube.com/watch?v=r5xe8ttPUXY ENJOY!

The History and Tradition of Peas 'N' Rice in Bahamian Cuisine

In June, after the rain, I often see friends sitting on their front porches shucking pigeon peas. What a delightful way to spend the day, chatting and learning the secrets of peas 'n' rice.

Peas 'n' rice holds a cherished place in Bahamian cuisine, capturing both the hearts and appetites of those who savor it. My friends and family adore this dish and could easily eat it daily. But there's more to peas 'n' rice than its mouthwatering taste; it's steeped in history and tradition that resonate deeply within Bahamian culture. Whether it's the hearty flavor of peas 'n' rice or the refreshing zest of conch salad, these dishes embody the essence of Bahamian culinary heritage, the rich tapestry of history and tradition making peas 'n' rice uniquely Bahamian.

Origins of the Dish

Peas 'n' rice is more than just a staple on the Bahamian table—it's a dish deeply rooted in the islands' history and culture. The origins of this savory delight stretch back to the late nineteenth century, when subsistence farming was essential, particularly in the Family Islands (all islands in the Bahamas apart from New Providence and Nassau). Most citizens engaged in outdoor labor, depending on the land for sustenance and survival.

The ingredients

Central to this historical cuisine were hardy pigeon pea plants and corn, harvested and ground into cornmeal grits. In a Bahamian field, you would find tall stalks of corn interspersed with vine plants like beans, okra, and tomatoes alongside large pigeon pea plants. These ingredients complemented each other marvelously, forming the backbone of what later evolved into Bahamian peas 'n' rice.

Early Adaptations

After the rainy season, locals harvested corn and pigeon peas sequentially, making them perfect companions in the kitchen. Initially prepared as a one-pot meal, the combination of cornmeal grits, pigeon peas, and any available meat or fish provided a nutritious and hearty meal. This early version of peas 'n' rice allowed islanders to thrive off locally farmed foods and served as an excellent source of nutrition for long days spent laboring in the fields.

Transition to Rice

Rice, a now universal component of Bahamian peas 'n' rice, wasn't always part of the dish. Since rice isn't cultivated in the Bahamas, its incorporation into the local cuisine only began in the early twentieth century, when imports from the American South introduced rice and other processed foods to the region. Before this transition, peas 'n' grits was the dish of choice, embodying the same essence but with locally available ingredients.

Evolution Over Time

Originally, peas 'n' rice was a one-pot meal with meat, vegetables, and starch, embodying the resourcefulness necessary for survival in the Bahamian islands. Over time, as the culinary landscape evolved, peas 'n' rice became a beloved side dish on the modern Bahamian plate, accompanying various main dishes but still holding onto its historical significance.

The Dish's Cultural Significance

Peas 'n' rice is not just food; it reflects Bahamian resilience, adaptability, and tradition. It is a culinary symbol of how the islanders made the most of what their environment could provide, blending imported influences while preserving local customs.

For Bahamian culture enthusiasts, culinary travelers, and history buffs alike, peas 'n' rice offers a delicious gateway into understanding the rich, vibrant history of the Bahamas. Each bite tells a story of survival, community, and the evolution of a nation's palate.

Dive into the flavors of history and enjoy a taste of Bahamian heritage with every peas 'n' rice mouthful.

Ingredients:

- 1 small onion
- 1 small, sweet pepper
- 1 tbsp cooking oil
- 2 strips of cooked bacon
- 2 tbsp tomato paste
- Three or four sprigs of fresh thyme
- Salt and red pepper to taste
- 1 tsp browning (optional)
- 1 chopped fresh tomato (optional)
- 1 large can of regular pigeon peas or pigeon peas in coconut milk
- 2 cups uncooked long grain white rice
- 3 cups water

Directions:

- Dice onion and sweet pepper
- In a hard-bottom pot, heat oil and fry onion, sweet pepper, and bacon along with the thyme
- Stir in tomato paste, add salt and pepper to taste (and optional browning and chopped tomato)
- Add the pigeon peas and stir well, then add water, bring to a boil, and season to taste
- Add the rice until it is about an inch and a half below the water line
- Stir well, lower the heat to medium with pot uncovered
- While the pot is simmering, stir at regular intervals
- When the rice has absorbed most of the water, turn the stove to low heat and cover the pot
- Leave to steam until fully cooked
- Enjoy with meat or fish

See more True Bahamian Recipes in the last chapter of this book.

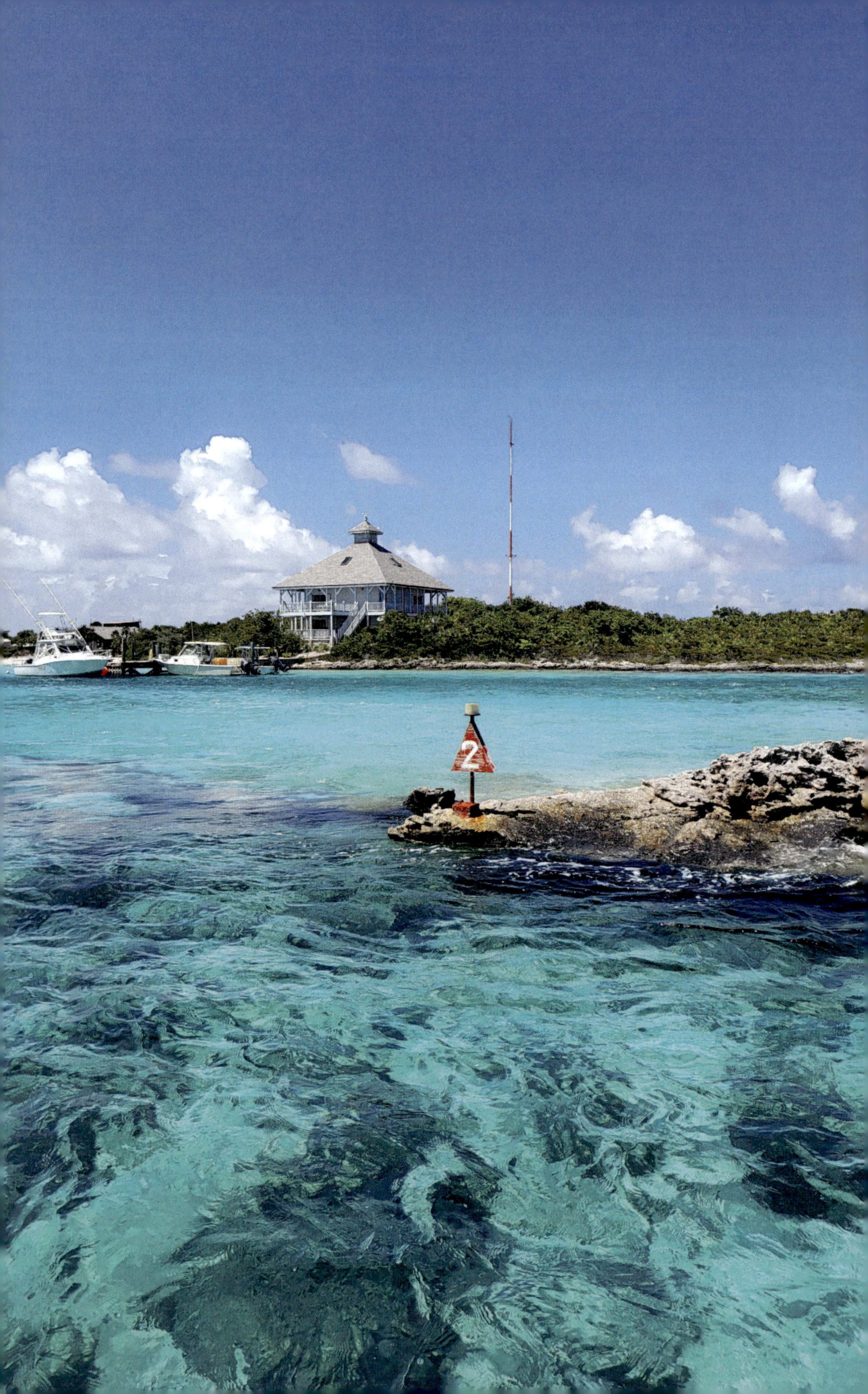
2

Chapter Five

Things to Do to Unleash Your Adventurous Side in Staniel and the Exuma Cays

Discover Staniel Cay and Explore the Exuma Cays

Are you ready for an unforgettable adventure? The Exuma Cays are calling your name! Whether you're an adrenaline junkie, nature enthusiast, or luxury traveler, the Exuma Cays offer a range of experiences that cater to all your adventurous desires. From pristine beaches and vibrant marine life to thrilling water sports and luxurious boat charters, there's something for everyone. Let's dive into what makes Staniel and the Exuma Cays the perfect choice for your next getaway.

My top choice for boating and exploring the Exuma Cays is Staniel Cay Adventures. With years of experience and a team of highly skilled tour guides, every trip with Staniel Cay Adventures promises to be memorable. They offer a variety of activities that will leave you exhilarated and longing for more. While Staniel Cay Adventures does not offer vacation rentals, they focus on and excel in providing guided tours and adventures. Their reputation for excellence makes them a trusted partner for your explorations. Each vacation rental provider has their service of choice for boating, tours, and fishing.

Adrenaline-Fueled Activities

For those seeking an adrenaline rush, the Exuma Cays offers:

- **Fishing.** No matter if you're an experienced or novice angler, the rich waters around Staniel Cay provide the perfect setting for a thrilling fishing adventure.
- **Scuba diving.** Discover the underwater wonders of the Exuma Cays. With crystal-clear waters and abundant marine life, scuba diving here is an experience like no other.
- **Snorkeling.** There are hundreds of incredible snorkeling areas for you to explore.

Luxurious Experiences

If luxury travel is more your style, Staniel Cay Adventures has you covered:

- **Private boat charters.** Explore the cays in style with a private boat charter. Enjoy a personalized experience tailored to your preferences, from secluded beach picnics to sunset cruises.

Ready to start your adventure?

Experience the Best of Staniel Cay Adventures

The Exuma Cays are a paradise waiting to be discovered, and Staniel Cay Adventures is my choice for a gateway to an unforgettable experience. Whether you're after high-octane adventures or luxurious relaxation, they have something for everyone. Don't miss out on the chance to make memories that will last a lifetime.

With years of experience and a team of highly skilled tour guides, every trip with Staniel Cay Adventures will be memorable. Here are two standout experiences to inspire your next adventure:

Brunch or Lunch in Paradise

One unforgettable day was when my son and a close friend surprised me with a Brunch or Lunch in Paradise. Partnering with the Staniel Cay Yacht Club, Staniel Cay Adventures set up an incredible dining experience on a secluded sandbar. Imagine having your feet in the water, with a personal server catering to your every drink or food desire. Beautiful tables, chairs, real dishes, and Bahamian decor added to the magic of the surprise. We enjoyed delicious food surrounded by stunning views and crystal-clear waters, played sandbar games, and dipped in the water between courses. It was indeed a slice of heaven!

The Bahamian Experience

Another unforgettable adventure was the Bahamian Experience, which I've cherished for over twenty-five years. This unique day involved catching, cleaning, and eating our fresh catch right on the beach. Conch salad, fresh fish, and some sides made for a memorable lunch! The skilled guides did all the hard work, leaving us to savor the freshest seafood imaginable. I still dream of those days filled with laughter, sunshine, and the taste of the sea.

Why I think choosing Staniel Cay Adventures is "The Ting to Do"?

- **Expertly guided tours.** Experience the Bahamas with knowledgeable local guides.
- **Variety of adventurous activities.** From snorkeling to island hopping, there's something for everyone.
- **Personalized experiences.** Tailor your trip to your preferences.
- **Partnerships with local establishments.** Enjoy exclusive experiences with reputable local partners.
- **Unforgettable memories.** Create stories you'll cherish forever.
- **Licensed and insured.** Enjoy peace of mind with a professional and reliable service.
- **Rave reviews.** Read hundreds of glowing reviews. At the time of this writing, only two reviews were less than five stars!

Reconnect with nature, experience the thrill, and indulge in luxury with Staniel Cay Adventures. Your dream adventure awaits.

Staniel Cay Adventures, www.stanielcayadventures.com, call at 242-524-8062, or email at info@stanielcayadventures.com.

Discover the Ultimate Fishing Adventure in the Exuma Cays

Imagine a paradise where crystal-clear waters meet vibrant marine life, creating a fishing enthusiast's dream. Welcome to the Exuma Cays, a stunning collection of over 365 Bahamas islands—an island for every day of the year and more beaches and sandbars than you can visit in two—renowned for their diverse fishing opportunities. Whether you're a seasoned angler or a vacationer eager to try fishing, the Exuma Cays offer an unparalleled experience. Let's explore various fishing styles and the best times to catch specific fish in this picturesque locale. Get ready for an adventure that combines relaxation, excitement, and the thrill of the catch.

The Allure of Fishing in the Exuma Cays

The Exuma Cays are a haven for fishing enthusiasts, offering a unique blend of beauty and biodiversity. The turquoise waters are home to various fish species, making it a prime destination for various fishing styles. But what makes fishing in the Exuma Cays so special?

First, the pristine environment provides an ideal habitat for fish, ensuring abundant catches. Second, the variety of fishing techniques available means there's something for everyone, regardless of skill level. Finally, the friendly local guides and charters enhance the experience, offering insider knowledge and unparalleled expertise.

Deep Drop Fishing

What is Deep Drop Fishing?

Deep drop fishing involves dropping bait to great depths, usually between 400 to 1,200 feet, to target deep-water species. This method requires specialized equipment, including electric reels and heavy weights, to reach the ocean floor.

Target Species

In the Exuma Cays, deep-drop fishing is gratifying. Anglers can expect to catch species such as:

- Queen Snapper
- Yellow-eye Snapper
- Silk Snapper
- Tilefish

Best Time to Go

While deep drop fishing can be productive year-round, the best time to target these deep-water species is during the cooler months, from November to April, when the water temperatures are optimal for deep-water fishing.

Deep Sea Fishing

The Thrill of the Open Ocean

Deep sea fishing, also known as offshore fishing, takes anglers far from the coast into waters hundreds of feet deep. This style of fishing is exhilarating, offering the chance to catch large, powerful fish.

Target Species

The species you can catch while deep sea fishing in the Exuma Cays are truly impressive. Some of the most sought-after fish include:

- Blue Marlin
- White Marlin
- Mahi-Mahi (Dolphin Fish)
- Wahoo
- Tuna

Seasonal Tips

The best time for deep sea fishing in the Exuma Cays is April to September. During these months, migratory species like marlin and tuna are most abundant, providing thrilling opportunities for anglers.

Handlining

A Traditional Approach

Handlining is a simple yet effective fishing method that involves using a line held in your hand rather than a rod and reel. This technique is deeply rooted in tradition and offers a more tactile fishing experience.

Target Species

Handlining in the Exuma Cays can yield a variety of smaller fish species, such as:

- Grunts
- Snappers
- Groupers

When to Handline

You can handline, but it's particularly enjoyable during the summer months when the weather is warm and the seas are calm. This method is perfect for those looking for a relaxed, hands-on fishing experience.

Spear Fishing

The Underwater Hunt

Spear fishing combines the thrill of hunting with the allure of the underwater world. Using a spear gun or pole spear, divers hunt fish while free-diving or snorkeling. This method requires skill and precision, but offers an incredibly rewarding experience.

Target Species

The Exuma Cays are a fantastic location for spearfishing, with species such as:

- Hogfish
- Lionfish
- Grouper
- Snapper

The Best Season

Spearfishing is best during the summer months, from May to September. The warm water temperatures and clear visibility make it easier to spot and hunt fish.

Bonefishing

The Art of the Flats

Bonefishing is a specialized type of fly-fishing that takes place in shallow, sandy flats. Bonefish are known for their speed and agility, making them a challenging and exciting target for anglers.

Target Species

In addition to bonefish, the flats of the Exuma Cays are home to other species, such as:

- Permit
- Tarpon
- Barracuda

Timing Your Trip

The best time for bonefishing in the Exuma Cays is during the spring and fall, from March to May and September to November. During these periods, the water temperatures are ideal, and fish are most active.

Fishing Charters

Guided Expertise

Booking a fishing charter in the Exuma Cays is a fantastic way to enhance your fishing experience. Local guides know the best spots, techniques, and times to fish, ensuring a successful and enjoyable outing.

What to Expect

A typical fishing charter includes:

- All necessary equipment
- Expert guidance
- Refreshments
- A memorable day on the water

Choosing the Right Charter

When selecting a local fishing charter, consider factors such as the fishing you want to do, the size of your group, and the reputation of the charter company. Reading reviews and asking for recommendations can help you make an informed decision. For example, are they licensed and insured?

Conservation and Sustainability

Responsible Fishing Practices

Fishing in the Exuma Cays is not just about the thrill of the catch; it's also about preserving the environment and ensuring sustainable practices. Responsible anglers follow guidelines to protect fish populations and their habitats.

Catch and Release

One of the most important practices is catch and release, particularly for species not intended for consumption. This practice helps maintain healthy fish populations and ensures future generations can enjoy the sport.

Supporting Local Communities

By choosing sustainable fishing practices and supporting local businesses, anglers can contribute to the conservation efforts in the Exuma Cays. This helps protect the natural beauty and biodiversity of the area.

Fishing Gear and Equipment

Essential Gear

Having the right gear is crucial for a successful fishing trip. Depending on the type of fishing you're doing, you may need:

- Rods and reels
- Lines and hooks
- Bait and lures
- Weights and bobbers

Advanced Equipment

For more specialized fishing, advanced equipment such as electric reels, spear guns, and fly-fishing rods may be necessary. Investing in high-quality gear can make a significant difference in your fishing experience.

Preparing for Your Trip

Packing Essentials

When preparing for a fishing trip to the Exuma Cays, pack essentials such as:

- Sunscreen

- Sunglasses
- Hat
- Lightweight UV protective clothing
- Water and snacks

Weather Considerations

Check the forecast before your trip and be prepared for changes in conditions. The tropical climate of the Exuma Cays can bring sudden rain showers, so having waterproof gear is advisable.

Travel Arrangements

Plan your travel arrangements in advance, including flights, accommodations, and transportation to fishing spots. Booking early can help secure the best deals and ensure a smooth trip.

Building Your Fishing Skills

Learn from Experts

Whether you're a beginner or an experienced angler, there's always something new to learn about fishing. Consider taking lessons or joining workshops led by local experts to improve your skills.

Practice Makes Perfect

The more you fish, the better you'll become. Practice different techniques and experiment with gear to find what works best for you. Patience and persistence are key to becoming a successful angler.

Joining Fishing Communities

Connecting with other fishing enthusiasts can provide valuable insights and support. Join online forums, social media groups, or local clubs to share experiences, ask questions, and stay updated on the latest fishing trends.

Exploring Beyond Fishing

Other Activities in the Exuma Cays

While fishing is a major attraction, the Exuma Cays offer plenty of other activities to enjoy, such as:

- Snorkeling and scuba diving
- Snorkeling in the aquarium
- Exuma Land and Sea Park
- Exploring Thunderball Grotto
- Relaxing on pristine beaches

Family-Friendly Options

The Exuma Cays are a great destination for families. In addition to fishing, kids and adults alike can enjoy boat tours, wildlife encounters, and water sports.

Savoring Local Cuisine

Don't miss the opportunity to sample the local Bahamian cuisine. Fresh seafood, conch fritters, and tropical fruits are just a few delicious options. Take your catch to a local restaurant, and they will prepare it!

Fishing in the Exuma Cays is an experience like no other. From deep drop and deep sea fishing to handlining and spearfishing, this paradise offers something for every angler. The beautiful environment, diverse fish species, and expert guidance ensure a memorable adventure.

Ready to cast your line in the Exuma Cays? Start planning your trip today and immerse yourself in the ultimate fishing experience. Whether you're looking to relax or reel in the big one, the Exuma Cays have it all. Happy fishing!

Discover the Thrills of Scuba Diving in the Exuma Cays

Are you ready to plunge into an underwater paradise? The Exuma Cays, with their vibrant marine life and stunning coral reefs, are calling your name. If you're a vacationer, adventure seeker, or scuba diving enthusiast looking for the next great licensed scuba diving company, pack your bags and head to the Exuma Cays.

Why Choose the Exuma Cays for Scuba Diving?

The Exuma Cays offer a unique combination of crystal-clear waters, diverse marine life, and stunning underwater landscapes. Whether you're a beginner or an advanced diver, there's something here for everyone.

A Diverse Range of Dives

From deep dives to shallow reef explorations, the Exuma Cays have it all. You can experience drift dives where the current carries you along, or face the exhilarating challenge of shark dives. The variety in Exuma Cay ensures that every dive feels like a new adventure.

Pristine Coral Reefs

One of the highlights of scuba diving in the Exuma Cays is the chance to explore pristine coral reefs. These underwater gardens are teeming with life, offering a kaleidoscope of colors and shapes that will take your breath away.

A few dive sites comprise beautiful, thriving sea walls such as the Whale Tail Wall, where eagle rays are often spotted, and Pillar Wall begins at 40 and drops over 333 feet, especially great for deep divers.

There is also a wreck you can dive around; the Austin Smith Wreck, lying 60 feet below sea level and about 82 feet long, has created a spectacular dive spot. If you seek even more excitement, then head to The Washing Machine, a place where the tide can make you tumble around, if you wish. If you would rather watch from the sidelines, it still has an impressive reef teeming with life. When it comes to reefs, the Amberjack Reef is a small patch of reef extraordinarily full of marine life, thousands of fish will surround you, and there are multiple reef sharks that call this reef their home.

Exclusive Diving Experiences

Staniel Cay Adventures is the only licensed scuba diving company in the Exuma Cays. They offer everything you need, from gear rentals to certified instructors and dive masters, ensuring a safe and unforgettable experience.

If you're new to scuba diving, or are looking to enhance your skills, Staniel Cay Adventures has you covered. Their experienced instructors will guide you through every step, ensuring you're comfortable and confident in the water.

Convenient Gear Rentals

Forget the hassle of bringing your own gear. Staniel Cay Adventures offers top-quality equipment rentals so you can focus on enjoying your dives.

Certified Instructors

Safety is paramount when it comes to scuba diving. That's why Staniel Cay Adventures employs certified instructors who are experts in their field. They'll ensure you have a safe and enjoyable experience, whether it's your first dive or your fiftieth.

Flexible Diving Options

No matter your skill level, Staniel Cay Adventures offer a range of dives to suit your needs. From beginner-friendly shallow dives to challenging deep dives, you can choose the right adventure for you.

Exploring the Exuma Land and Sea Park

Exuma Land and Sea Park is a protected area that offers some of the best scuba diving spots in the region. There is a fee to enter the park. Just check in at Warderick Wells or find a pay box. Here's what you can expect when you explore this underwater wonderland. See the dedicated chapter on the park to learn more about their above water adventures.

Shallow Reef Dives

Shallow reef dives are perfect for beginners or those who want a more relaxed experience. You can swim alongside colorful fish and marvel at the beauty of the coral formations.

Deep Dives

For the more adventurous, deep dives offer a thrilling experience. Descend into the depths and discover a world few get to see. The deeper you go, the more unique and fascinating the marine life becomes.

Drift Dives

Drift dives are a unique experience where the current does most of the work. You'll feel like you're flying as the water carries you along, allowing you to cover more ground and see a variety of underwater landscapes.

The Marine Life of the Exumas

The Exuma Cays are home to a rich diversity of marine life. Here's a glimpse of what you might encounter on your dives.

Colorful Reef Inhabitants

The coral reefs are bustling with life. Schools of vibrant fish dart in and out of the coral, while larger species like barracudas and groupers patrol the waters. Every dive offers the chance to see something new and exciting.

Exotic Aquatic Species

The waters around the Exuma Cays are home to species you won't find anywhere else. From rare fish to unique coral formations, the underwater world is truly one-of-a-kind.

Sharks and Rays

For those seeking a bit more adrenaline, the Exuma Cays offer the chance to swim with sharks and rays. These majestic creatures are often misunderstood, but seeing them in their natural habitat is an awe-inspiring experience.

Tips for a Successful Diving Trip

To make the most of your scuba diving adventure in the Exuma Cays, here are some tips to keep in mind.

Plan Ahead

Booking your dives in advance ensures you get the dates and times that work best for you. This is especially important during peak travel seasons.

Stay Hydrated

Diving can dehydrate you, so it's important to drink plenty of water before and after your dives. Doing so will help you stay focused and energized.

Respect the Environment

Always follow the guidance of your instructors/guides and respect the marine environment. Avoid touching the coral or disturbing the wildlife to help preserve the beauty of the Exuma Cays for future generations.

Share Your Experiences

After your dives, share your experiences with other divers. Swap stories, tips, and photos to make the most of your trip.

Scuba diving in the Exuma Cays is an experience like no other. With its diverse marine life, stunning coral reefs, and exclusive diving options, it's the perfect destination for vacationers, adventure seekers, and scuba enthusiasts alike.

Discover why the Exuma Cays are a diver's paradise. Your underwater adventure awaits!

Staniel Cay Adventures

Scuba Diving Equipment Rental

Group or Private Dive: includes Scuba Pro BCD, regulator, mask, snorkel, fins, weight belt, weights, and tanks.

Equipment Rental

- **BCD**
- **Regulator**
- **Dive computer**
- **Mask, fins, and snorkel**
- **Tank:**
- **Tank fills**

ADI Discover Scuba Diving Information

- **PADI Discover Scuba Diving**
- **Optional:** Open water dive two open water dives
- **Course time:** One day (1 hour)
- **Content:** One academic module, one confined open water session, optional open water dive

- **Maximum depth allowed:** 12 meters/40 feet, under a PADI professional's supervision
- **Prerequisites:** Ten years old and up, no previous experience necessary
- **Note:** Maximum is three non-certified divers to go on an open water dive per dive instructor. When grouping non-certified and certified divers, they can carry four divers max per dive instructor
- **Course package includes:** All materials and equipment

For any questions or concerns you may have about scuba diving on Staniel Cay, please email them at: dive@stanielcayadventures.com, call 242-524-8062, or visit their website at www.stanielcayadventures.com

The Hidden Gems of Staniel Cay's Beaches

Staniel Cay offers a much-needed respite for those looking to escape the popular destinations' crowded beaches and tourist traps. This charming little island and the surrounding area are home to some of the world's most breathtakingly beautiful beaches and sandbars. Staniel Cay has everything from seclusion and serenity to vibrant colors and diverse marine life. Let's explore some of the hidden gems of Staniel Cay's beaches.

Hidden Serenity: Ho Tai Cay Beach Whispers Tranquility

Craving a slice of paradise far from the tourist throngs? Look no further than Ho Tai Cay Beach, a secluded gem nestled within a cove on Staniel Cay. Bordered by lush ridges and embraced by the open water, this beach offers a unique escape for those seeking solitude. Forget crowded shores; here, your day unfolds amid the rhythm of lapping waves and the whisper of the wind.

Forget lounging on sand in a bustling crowd. Ho Tai Cay Beach is a place to connect with nature's true beauty. Immerse yourself in the pristine waters, their crystal clarity revealing a vibrant underwater world. Let the sun warm your skin as you bask on the shore, serenaded by the gentle ocean breeze. This untouched haven whispers peace, allowing you to unwind and find yourself truly.

While the beach provides tranquility, its location adds another layer of intrigue. Sheltered by the channel dividing the ocean ridge and Staniel Cay, Ho Tai Cay Beach enjoys calmer waters, becoming a hidden oasis for locals seeking festive gatherings. This duality adds a touch of charm, hinting at the vibrant life surrounding your peaceful haven. So, escape the ordinary and discover the magic of Ho Tai Cay Beach—a sanctuary of serenity waiting to be explored.

Adventure Awaits: Pirate's Beach at the Northern Tip of the Island

Pirate's Beach, set at the island's northernmost point, isn't just another sun-kissed haven; it's an adventure waiting to be explored. Rugged and untamed, it embodies the island's natural spirit. Unique rock formations rise like silent sentinels at the back, whispering tales of undiscovered coves and hidden treasures. Dive into the crystal-clear waters and let the kaleidoscope of fish swirling around vibrant coral reefs dazzle you.

But heed the call of caution! Powerful currents guard the channel, and passing boats demand respect. Pirate's Beach may not be the gentlest stretch of sand, but it's a hidden gem waiting to be unearthed for those seeking a wilder, more exhilarating experience.

Expansive Ocean Views: Ocean Beach Over the Ridge

On the far side of the ridge, Ocean Beach on Staniel Cay is the perfect choice if you're seeking a beach with vibrant colors that leaves you in awe of nature's beauty. The dramatic waves and sunrise views that make up this beach create an unforgettable scene.

Waves crash into the soft sands, making them a perfect place to sunbathe, walk, or play. Relax and soak up some sun while basking in the beauty of this natural wonder.

Whether you're looking for a place to relax and unwind or for an adventure-filled day, Ocean Beach will indeed please.

Staniel Cay Town Beach: A Paradise for Relaxation and Family Fun

Stretching out in the heart of Staniel Cay, the beach isn't just a scenic escape; it's a vibrant hub for fun in the sun. Imagine soaking up the warmth on pristine white sand, turquoise waters lapping gently at your toes. Perfect for families, the beach boasts shallow, crystal-clear waters, creating a haven for little ones to splash and play, build sandcastles, collect seashells, or relax under the swaying pine and palm trees—endless possibilities.

But the fun doesn't stop there! With its central location, charming restaurants and inviting shops within a short walk surround the beach. Indulge in fresh, local seafood after a refreshing swim, or browse for souvenirs to remember your island adventure. Visit the Liquor mart or Lindsley Boutique and spend the entire day there, seamlessly transitioning from beach bliss to culinary delights and retail therapy without venturing far. Staniel Cay Town Beach offers the perfect blend of relaxation, recreation, and convenience, making it a must-stop on your island getaway.

Adventure Awaits: Sunken Plane Just off Toms Cay

While most may head straight for the swimming pigs, Staniel Cay boasts another intriguing attraction: a sunken plane! This underwater marvel awaits exploration on the far side of Toms Cay, near the government dock. Whether you're a seasoned or first-time snorkeler, the shallow, crystal-clear waters surrounding the wreck promise an unforgettable experience.

Dive in and let a vibrant marine oasis greet you. Schools of brightly colored fish flit among the plane's remains, an artificial reef teeming with life. Keep your eyes peeled for playful stingrays gliding across the sandy bottom, or perhaps a majestic sea turtle swimming through the underwater landscape. This sunken treasure offers a unique glimpse into the underwater world, combining history, adventure, and stunning natural beauty. So, take advantage of the chance to explore this sunken gem during your Staniel Cay adventure!

The beaches of Staniel Cay are treasures. They're an oasis of solitude, beauty, vibrant color, adventure, and marine life. They offer everything from seclusion to action-packed water sports. Whether you want to spend the day lounging on the sand, snorkeling, fishing, or playing with your family, a beach is perfect for you. The thing you won't want to miss on Staniel Cay is an opportunity to disconnect from the hustle and bustle of everyday life and immerse yourself in the splendor of the natural world. So, book your trip to Staniel Cay and experience it for yourself.

Let's Go Crabbing!

Listen to Elon Moxey "Catch da Crab" on YouTube https://www.youtube.com/watch?v=GRTUly8LEd0

Elon Moxey is a Bahamian Rake-and-scrape artist, nationally acclaimed in the Bahamas.

When crab season is in full swing, there's no better place to experience this unique adventure than in the Bahamas. Whether you're a nature lover or a seafood enthusiast, crabbing offers an exciting way to connect with the environment and enjoy fresh catches. Let's explore the world of crabbing in the Bahamas. The biggest island in the Bahamas, Andros, has an abundant population of free-roaming land crabs. I learned to crab in the Abcos but have caught them on Staniel Cay and in the Ragged Islands.

The Crabbing Season

Mid-August is a perfect time for crabbing. The behavior you may witness during this period is part of the land crab's fascinating life cycle. These crabs live on land, mainly burrowing in muddy areas where water saturates the soil and rock. Crabbing season typically starts when the heavy rains pour, usually in late May or early June.

The Land Crab Life Cycle

Here's a quick breakdown of the land crab's life cycle:

1. **Mating season.** During the heavy rains, land crabs mate.
2. **Egg fertilization.** About two weeks after mating, the females' eggs fertilize.
3. **Migration to the ocean.** To release their eggs into the saltwater, female crabs migrate from land to the ocean.

Understanding this life cycle can make your crabbing experience even more enriching. It's amazing to see how these creatures adapt and thrive in their natural habitat.

Crabbing on any island

The island's environment is perfect for land crabs, as it offers plenty of muddy areas for burrowing. Here's what you need to know about crabbing:

Best Spots for Crabbing

The island has many spots where you can find land crabs. Look for areas with:

1. Muddy soil and rocks saturated with water

2. Nearby saltwater access
3. Heavy vegetation provides cover

Gear and Techniques

Before heading out, ensure you have the right gear:

- **Potato or onion sack.** Useful for catching crabs and placing them inside quickly.
- A small fishing net or learn how to stop crabs gently with your foot and pick them up with your hand without getting pinched/bitten.
- **Flashlights.** Essential for night crabbing.
- LOTS of bug-repellant.
- Wear long sleeves, pants, and closed-toe shoes. You will run into spider webs!

When crabbing, remember to:

- Move slowly and quietly to avoid startling the crabs.
- Use your flashlight to spot crabs hiding in the mud and shine it in their eyes to stop them in their tracks.
- Gently scoop them up with your net and place them in your sack.

Responsible Crabbing

While crabbing is fun, it's important to practice responsible crabbing to protect the ecosystem:

- **Only take what you need.** Avoid overharvesting to ensure the crab population remains healthy. If you will not clean them to eat, give them to a local who will.
- **Handle crabs gently.** Release any unwanted crabs back into their habitat unharmed.
- **Respect local regulations.** Follow any guidelines set by local authorities to preserve the environment.

Crabbing in the Bahamas offers an unforgettable experience for nature lovers and seafood enthusiasts. By understanding the crabs' life cycle and practicing responsible crabbing, you can enjoy this activity while contributing to the preservation of the ecosystem.

Are you ready to go crabbing tonight? Pack your gear, head to the islands, and immerse yourself in this thrilling adventure. When you return home, place them in a pen away from the bright light, feed them cooked white rice and lettuce for a few days to clean them out and fatten them up.

If you're still curious about the best spots or need tips on techniques, connect with local experts who can enhance your crabbing experience. Enjoy the thrill of the catch and the beauty of the Bahamas!

Happy crabbing! Time to make some crab 'n' rice or stuffed crab.

Conclusion

In conclusion, Staniel Cay offers an array of diverse and captivating beaches, each with its own unique charm and allure. From the tranquil hideaway of Ho Tai Cay Beach, where the whisper of the wind and the lapping of waves offer a serene escape, to the adventurous allure of Pirate's Beach, where rugged beauty and challenging currents promise excitement for the daring traveler. Ocean Beach dazzles with its expansive views and dramatic colors, providing the perfect backdrop for both relaxation and adventure. Meanwhile, Staniel Cay Town Beach invites families to enjoy fun-filled days in the sun, surrounded by the vibrant local culture and amenities.

No matter what you seek—solitude, adventure, family fun, or scenic beauty—Staniel Cay's beaches promise unforgettable experiences. Whether lounging on secluded shores, exploring hidden coves, or basking in the island's lively ambiance, your island getaway is sure to be filled with memories to cherish. Discover the magic of Staniel Cay, where every beach tells its own story and adventure awaits at every turn.

Festive Spirit of the Exuma Cays: A Calendar of Celebrations

The sparkling turquoise waters and powdery beaches of the Exuma Cays are not the only reasons visitors flock to this enchanting archipelago within the Bahamas. The rich tapestry of holidays and celebrations adds a distinct flavor to the islands, infusing the tropical paradise with cultural vitality and excitement.

As vivid as the underwater coral gardens, the calendar of festivities in the Exuma Cays paints every season with vibrant colors of tradition, heritage, and jubilation. Whether you're a dedicated travel enthusiast, a holiday seeker, or an Exuma Cays explorer, understanding the local calendar guarantees a richer, more immersive journey. Here's your guide to navigating the highs of the holiday season in the Exuma Cays.

Embracing Local Traditions: When Every Day is a Celebration

Holidays on a weekend. In the Bahamas, the joy doesn't stop just because a holiday falls over the weekend. With a flexible calendar, there's always time for celebration. Holidays on a Saturday or Sunday move to the following Monday, ensuring no moment for festivity slips away.

Mid-week merriments. True to the island's leisurely pace, holidays falling on Wednesdays or Thursdays often see celebratory events shifted to the upcoming Friday. However, significant dates like Independence Day, Christmas, and Boxing Day hold their ground, steadfast in their mid-week revelry.

Exuma Cays Holiday and Events Calendar

- **January 1st: New Year's Day**

    Usher in the new year with Junkanoo parades—a festival of costume, dance, and vibrant music that's quintessentially Bahamian You will find the parades in Nassau and locals often leave the islands to join in the fun.

- **February: Staniel Cay Yacht Club Wahoo Blitz and Super Bowl Party**

    Visit their website for details: www.StanielCay.com.

- **March: The Spring Regatta**

    While not an official public holiday, it is the National Event. The National Family Island Regatta in late March is a high point in the Exuma calendar, drawing sailing enthusiasts from all corners of the globe.

- **St. Patrick's Day parties are at various clubs and restaurants on Staniel Cay and Black Point.**

- **Third Weekend in March: James Bond Casino Royale Party at the Staniel Cay Yacht Club**

    A fun weekend! *(Note: If Easter Sunday falls on the third weekend, the party will move to the SECOND weekend of March.)* The Staniel Cay Yacht Club transforms into an exhilarating world of espionage and elegance with its Annual James Bond Casino Royale Costume Party. A weekend filled with intrigue, sophistication, and non-stop entertainment, this event is a must-attend for thrill-seekers and fans of the iconic film franchise.

- **Easter Weekend**

    Good Friday and Easter Monday bookend a sacred weekend with religious observances and community activities, including the much-anticipated Easter Regatta.

- **Staniel Cay Yacht Club for the Little Explorers:**

    Our cherished annual Easter event promises an exhilarating quest for children aged ten and under. Watch their eyes light with games, crafts, and treats around the Staniel Cay Yacht Club. This lively search is more than just fun—it's a passport to make joyful Easter memories.

- **Tony Grey Sailing Club Event**

    (Check with locals for the date)

- **May 5: Cinco De Mayo! Staniel Cay Yacht Club**

- **First Friday in June: Labour Day**

    Labour Day unites the islands in a celebration of solidarity and hard work, featuring colorful parades and family picnics.

- **Whit Monday**

  Also known as Pentecost Monday, Whit Monday is a public holiday in several countries on the Monday after **Whitsunday**. Also known as **Pentecost or Whitsun**, Whitsunday is observed fifty days (roughly seven weeks) after Easter and ten days after Ascension. It marks the end of the Easter cycle, which began ninety days prior with Ash Wednesday at the start of Lent. Seven weeks after Easter, Whit Monday shines a light on the spiritual community with church services and peaceful reflection.

- **July 4th**

  Immerse yourself in the vibrancy and excitement at Staniel Cay Yacht Club! Elevate your Independence Day celebrations with an exhilarating Long Drive Contest, complimented by an exclusive Mimosa and Bloody Mary bar, to kick-start your day with flavor and fun. Worried about your golf balls plunging into the watery abyss? Fear not! Our dedicated distance spotters aboard boats will retrieve every single one, ensuring the fun remains uninterrupted.

  But that's just the beginning. Prepare yourself for a culinary voyage with their specially curated dinner, a gastronomic experience designed to tantalize your taste buds. And what better way to digest that feast than with the spectacular fireworks lighting up the night sky, setting the stage for an evening filled with awe and wonder? And the cherry on top? Live music and or DJ that promises to keep you on your feet, dancing and grooving into the night.

  However, seating at this premier event is limited. To ensure your place in this unforgettable celebration, reserve your spot. Simply email them at Dining@stanielcay.com.

- **July 10th: Independence Day**

  A date emblazoned in every Bahamian heart; Independence Day is the pinnacle of national pride. The islands erupt in a spectacle of events, fireworks, and cultural shows.

- **First Monday in August: Emancipation Day**

  Commemorating the abolition of slavery, Emancipation Day is both a somber reflection and an exultant celebration of freedom.

- **Second Monday in October: National Heroes Day**

  A salute to the Bahamian stalwarts. This day honors those who've shaped the nation's destiny, celebrated with ceremonies and community awards.

- **December 25th & 26th: Christmas and Boxing Day**

  These back-to-back holidays are a family-centric time of church services, feasting, and gift-giving, enveloped in a tropical Christmas charm.

- **December 28th**

  Set sail for the exclusive Lil' Mateys event at the illustrious Staniel Cay Yacht Club, where the most luxurious tiny pirates gather. From 4:00 to 6:00 p.m. your little ones can revel in an enchanted evening filled with captivating pirate crafts, enthralling games, and a treasure trove of gleaming riches tailored for our miniature swashbucklers. Indulge in the delight as your cherished tykes immerse themselves in the grandeur of the Lil' Mateys Lair, a sanctuary designed for pursuing adventure and discovery. It's an opportunity for them to forge their own legends in an atmosphere of refined fun and sophistication. Should you wish to partake in the joy and contribute your touch of magic to this splendid affair, consider volunteering your time to enrich their experience. Your esteemed contribution would be most welcome. Please express your interest in assisting at this noble gathering by inquiring within the hallowed halls of the SCYC Bar or by sending a missive to volunteer@stanielcay.com. Prepare to set a course for a captivating voyage under the azure skies—your Lil' Mateys rendezvous awaits, only at Staniel Cay Yacht Club. For more details, visit www.stanielcay.com.

- **December 28th Annual Pirate Party at Staniel cay Yacht Club.**

  Set sail for adventure and anchor down at the most swashbuckling soiree of the season! Don your most extravagant pirate attire and join us for an evening where the waves of merriment and the winds of festivity meet. A DJ will commandeer the tunes, ensuring the deck is awash with dance and revelry. Immerse in the spirit of the seven seas as we celebrate the age of buccaneers with a modern twist—an escapade that even the most discerning of voyageurs will treasure. Behold, prestigious awards await the crew with the most captivating costumes! Deck yourself in your finest pirate's garb, and you could walk away with more than just storied memories. My favorite party of the year and as big as New Year's Eve! For more details visit www.stanielcay.com.

- **December 29: Longest Drive**

  Unleash your inner golfer against the backdrop of a crisp sunrise at our exclusive Beachfront Golf Experience. At 10:00 a.m. sharp, engage in a leisurely morning of driving eco-friendly golf balls into the welcoming azure expanse. Venture beyond the ordinary as you soak in the warmth of the sun, the gentle sea breeze, and the sound of waves harmonizing with your every swing. Your $10 entry not only places you amidst fellow enthusiasts but also grants you a pass to the delectable Bloody Mary and Mimosa Bar—because what's a morning on the beach without a toast to the good life?

- **December 31st: New Year's Eve Celebration**

  Visit the Staniel Cay Yacht Club New Year's Eve Party to ring in the new year with friends new and old.

Seasonal and Observational Events

- **Mothers' and Valentine's Day:**

  While not public holidays, these days of observance are warmly honored with community events and special church services.

- **Celebrating Time: Daylight Savings Transitions**

  Whether springing forward or falling back, the Exuma Cays acknowledge these clock changes casually, allowing islanders and guests alike to acclimate at their leisurely island pace.

The Exuma Cays offer a destination and a festive journey through a cultural calendar as radiant as the Bahamian sun. From the heritage-heavy Independence Day to the joyous explosion of Junkanoo, a trip here isn't just a getaway—it's a leap into an ever-unfolding celebration. When you set sail for the Exuma Cays, you're joining a year-round festival brimming with Bahamian zest.

Beginners and seasoned travelers alike know that visiting the Exuma Cays is to step into a narrative of celebration. It's here, in the heart of the Bahamas, where every day is woven with the threads of observance, remembrance, and pure, unadulterated delight.

Are you ready to sync your heartbeat with the pulsing rhythms of the Exuma Cays' festive calendar? Plan your trip around these cultural high points and dive deep into the Bahamian spirit!

Staniel Cay Unveiled

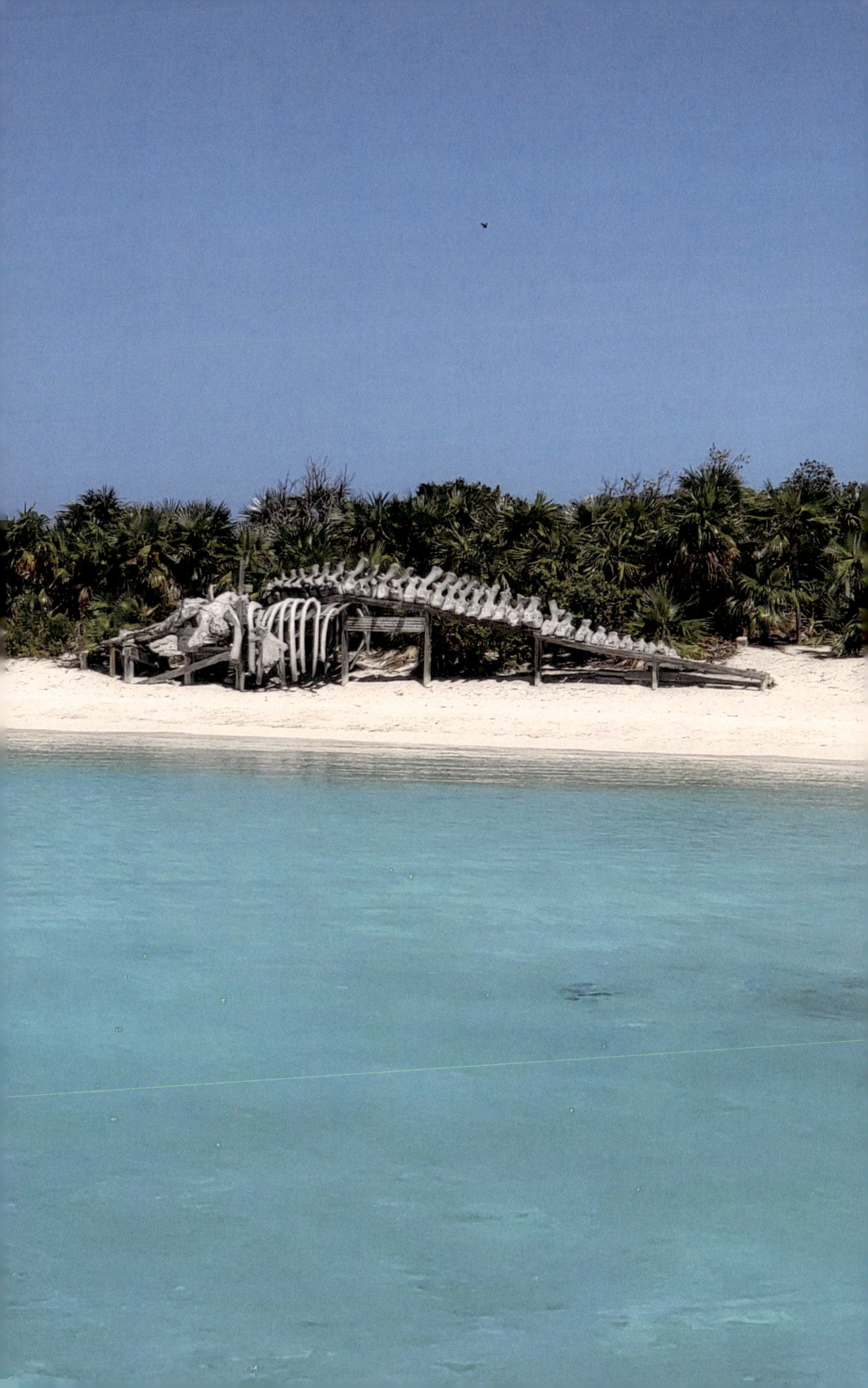

CHAPTER Six

Exploring the Staniel Cay: Event Services, Boats, Golf Carts, Water Toys, Snorkeling, and Diving Equipment on Staniel Cay

Please note WhatsApp is a standard for communication in the Cays. If the number starts with 242, try dialing it on WhatsApp first to save on international dialing rates.

The Exuma Cays are known for its crystal-clear waters, pristine beaches, and captivating marine life. You will want the right equipment and transportation to get the most out of exploring these breathtaking sights. Fortunately, Staniel Cay offers various rental options for those who'd prefer to explore the island at their own pace. Whether you are planning a romantic getaway, family vacation, wedding, or other special event, this chapter will provide you with vacation rentals, event services, rental boats, golf carts, snorkeling, and diving equipment on Staniel Cay, which can enhance your experience and save some packing.

Renting Boats on Staniel Cay: Safe and Fun Exploration

Staniel Cay has always been a popular tourist destination, and it's no surprise why. The pristine blue waters and stunning beaches provide an unparalleled experience, making it a must-visit place for every traveler. But if you want to explore Staniel Cay and the surrounding islands at your own pace, renting a boat is an excellent option.

The Basics of Renting Boats on Staniel Cay and How to Ensure a Safe and Fun Exploration

Renting a boat on Staniel Cay is an experience that will leave you with the ultimate feeling of freedom. But before renting a boat, it's imperative to understand that navigating the waters takes work. Hence, it's essential to pack essential gear, including a GPS, or hire a guide to help you navigate the waters. Make certain you charged your cell phone and keep in mind that some areas do not have cell service! Once you have that sorted, it's time to choose the right boat for your journey. At Staniel Cay, you can find boats varying in size and capacity. From small boats that can accommodate one to four people to larger boats that can carry ten to twelve people, you can choose one according to your needs and boating skills.

Once you have rented the perfect boat, it's time to pack your essentials. Remember to bring enough water (always more than you think you need), sunscreen, a long sleeve sun shirt, hat, a cooler, and ice for your excursion. My best advice is to take more than you need; I am known for being an ice lover, and my boys would always tease me, but they quickly learned that boating is no fun without something cool to drink or if their beer gets warm! The best part of renting a boat is that you can discover secluded beaches and hidden coves not accessible by land, making for a perfect picnic spot. Take advantage of the tranquil surroundings and delve deep into the island life. I'll say it again: there are 365 islands and Cays and more beaches and sandbars than you can visit in a year.

One of the most crucial aspects of boating is learning how to navigate unfamiliar waters. Understanding how to read the water can help you stay safe and navigate efficiently. Remember, "Brown, brown, run aground." If you see brown water, avoid it, as it might indicate coral reefs or rocks near the surface. However, white water means a shallow area with a sandy bottom, and green water indicates deeper waters. Last, blue water provides the safest passage. Following these simple guidelines, you can quickly navigate unfamiliar waters and keep your boat and passengers safe. The crystal-clear water can be intimidating because you can be in ten feet of water and think it's three feet. Same goes the other way around.

Safety should always be your top priority when venturing into water. Before embarking on your boating adventure, check for life jackets, safety gear, and first aid kits onboard. Checking the weather forecast is essential to ensure a safe journey. **Always let someone know about your plans and your expected return time**. This way, someone will know when to call for help if you don't return. And always follow all the safety regulations and guidelines while operating your boat and ensure you're well-prepared for emergencies.

Staniel Cay offers an incredible boating experience you shouldn't miss! Renting a boat is a convenient and safe way to explore the nearby islands and experience the best the Bahamas offer. With calm waters, pristine beaches, and stunning landscapes, Staniel Cay will leave you awestruck and craving more. Remember to pack your essentials, read the waters, and always prioritize safety. We hope this section will help you have a safe, stress-free, and fun-filled boating experience on your next trip to Staniel Cay. Happy exploring!

Renting Golf Carts:

Driving in the Bahamas: Why They Drive on the Left Side of the Road

If you plan to visit the Bahamas, you may wonder about the driving laws and rules. Different from many countries, Bahamians drive on the left side of the road, which can confuse first-time visitors. But why do they drive on the left side of the road? There is a fascinating history behind this driving convention in the Bahamas.

One of the reasons Bahamians drive on the left side of the road goes back to the British colonial days. The British Empire ruled over many countries, including the Bahamas, and they established the left-side driving convention, as it was common in Great Britain. As a result, many British Empire countries also drive on the left side of the road, including Australia, India, and South Africa.

Another theory behind the convention of left-side driving in the Bahamas relates to how people rode horses in the past. In medieval times, knights would ride their horses on the left side of the road, so their swords, kept on their left hip, wouldn't hit the person passing by on the right. This tradition may have influenced how we drive today, and some countries, like the Bahamas, have maintained this convention since then.

Interestingly enough, many countries in the world used to drive on the left side of the road, but the convention gradually shifted toward right-side driving. One reason for this change was the invention of the automobile. As cars became more popular, manufacturers started producing right-hand drive cars, making driving easier on the right side of the road. This led to most countries adopting right-side driving, while a few, like the Bahamas, maintained the original left-side driving convention.

If you're planning on driving in the Bahamas, keep a few tips in mind. First, remember the driver's seat is on the right side of the car, and you'll need to drive on the left side of the road. If you're not used to it, this can be challenging, so take your time and drive slowly. Also, remember that there are many roundabouts in the Bahamas, and traffic can be heavy in some areas, especially during rush hour at the airport. Staniel Cay will have a few cars and trucks on the roads, with the primary mode of transportation being golf carts. The roundabout by the airport is essential to understand, as it is shaped like a heart. Follow the markings on the road. Second, you must have a valid license to drive a golf cart with you at all times, and each rental company will have rules based on insurance requirements. Most have a driving age of twenty-one.

The history behind why the Bahamas drives on the left side of the road is fascinating. From medieval knights to British colonialism, there are many theories about the establishment of the convention. Regardless of the reason, if you're planning on driving in the Bahamas, it's essential to keep this driving convention in mind and take the time to get used to it. Remember, safety should always be your top priority, and follow all traffic laws and rules when on the road.

Safe travels!

Sun, Sand, and Sea Rentals: 242-808-6087 Full day $75, Half Day $60, and 1 hour $30.

EMBRACE Resort Golf Cart Rentals—https://stanielcayvacations.com/activities/stanielcaygolfcarts WhatsApp 242-524-0951**Cell:** 242-524- 7447 **Email:** info@embraceresort.com

Isles Inn Resort—**Golf Cart & Boat Rentals**—https://www.islesinnresort.com/golfcart-rentals **Contact person:** Vivian Rolle **Phone:** +1-242-355-2007 **Email:** rollesroost@batelnet.bs

Staniel Cay Golf Cart and Bike Rentals—https://stanielcaygolf-carts.com/ **Phone number** 242-447-8677 242-357-7761 **Email address:** carlosrolle8@gmail.com

Boat Rental: Dreko Chamberlain 1-242-359-1573

Boat Rentals with a Captain: Staniel Cay Adventures 242-524-8062 info@stanielcayadventures.com

Renting Snorkeling or Scuba Diving Equipment:

The Bahamas is known for its world-class snorkeling sites, and Staniel Cay is undoubtedly one of them. Renting snorkeling equipment is highly recommended if you want to explore the vibrant marine ecosystem surrounding the island. You can rent snorkel gear from the rental shop, which typically provides fins, masks, and snorkel tubes. Be sure to visit Thunderball Grotto, a popular snorkeling destination where you can swim through underwater tunnels and observe various marine life. They also offer beach chairs, umbrellas, beach toys, and fishing gear.

Staniel Cay offers excellent diving opportunities for avid divers. If you're a beginner, you can opt for a guided dive with a local dive shop offering trained instructors and certification courses. For experienced divers, famous sites like the Fowl Cay Marine Reserve, Rocky Dundas, and the Austin Smith Wreck offer stunning underwater topography and marine biodiversity. Renting diving equipment is an excellent way to explore these sought-after diving destinations.

Staniel Cay Adventures: https://stanielcayadventures.com info@StanielCayAdventures.com Text or Call (242) 524-8062 and What's App. On Main Street, beachside, second building on the right when leaving the Yacht Club. The building is covered in white native stone.

Planning your Rentals:

Planning is essential to ensure you get the desired boat or golf cart rental. It's best to book your rentals by calling or booking online in advance to secure them, especially during the peak season. You need to pay a deposit and reconfirm your reservation before arriving. My advice is to make it your responsibility to pay the deposit and get a letter or receipt, especially when renting a golf cart or boat. This island is tiny; without payment, you do not have a reservation. Rental prices usually vary depending on the equipment and the rental duration. Review the equipment condition and safety instructions provided by the rental company.

Staniel Cay's rental options offer a fantastic way to explore the island and its surrounding attractions. Keep in mind that it is a trendy travel destination. Whether you want to explore the nearby islands on a boat, soak up the sun on a scenic beach with your rented golf cart, or delve into the vibrant underwater world with snorkeling or diving gear, Staniel Cay offers something for every traveler. Renting equipment allows you to create your adventure schedule and enjoy the Bahamas your way.

Planning Your Event, Party or Special Moment:

Airbourn Creations

They will transform your events into unforgettable experiences with exquisite balloon decor and arrangement expertise. From elegant balloon arches to whimsical balloon bouquets, they specialize in creating stunning designs tailored to your specific event. Whether you're hosting an intimate setting or a grand celebration, our decorations will leave a lasting impression. Custom Creations for Milestone birthdays, weddings, and corporate events—no matter the occasion, we offer personalized balloon decor that will make your event truly special. Their custom creations are designed to reflect your unique style and vision.

They offer Delivery & Setup Sit back and relax! We handle the setup and delivery, ensuring everything is perfect for your big day. Our team is dedicated to ensuring every detail is just right so you can focus on enjoying the event.

Contact: Visit https://airbornecreations.org/ or call Shoron Rolle at 1-242-395-3132 and the same number on WhatsApp.

Photography: Bernadette Chamberlain

Traditional Junkanoo Band and other music: Contact Rashaun Rolle at 242-524-8156 also on WhatsApp or email at Rashaunr@hotmail.com

Hair, Massages, Manicures, Pedicures and Nails: Contact Kori

Rent A Private Island For the Day

Brunch or Lunch In Paradise

A True Bahamian Beach Picnic Day

Planning a destination wedding can be overwhelming, our goal is to make it easy. Find the answers you need to the most frequently asked questions, from marriage license requirements to officiant logistics. You can also contact one of our Romance Specialists. They're here to ease your concerns every step of the way - from wedding and reception venues to planning your honeymoon and all the details in between.

FAQ &b Information https://www.bahamas.com/plan-your-trip/weddings/marriage-license

Weddings & Private Events Staniel Cay Yacht Club: https://stanielcay.com/activ.../weddings-and-private-events/

Wedding Planning Services 3 N's: https://stanielcayvacations.com/weddings/

EXUMA CAYS
LAND AND SEA PARK

CHAPTER *Seven*

Dining Options on Staniel Cay and Other Cays Nearby

When it comes to dining on Staniel Cay, the Exuma Cays have a few options that cater to different tastes and budgets. You'll find something to satisfy your cravings: simple food and gourmet cuisine. Remember, since everything is either boated in or flown in, prices can cause sticker shock. Visit one of the grocery stores and you will learn quickly the cost of living on a small remote island.

Experience the Best of Staniel Cay with Exceptional Private Catering

Savor Home-Cooked Meals in Paradise

Are you visiting Staniel Cay and craving a delicious, home-cooked meal? Look no further! Enhance your stay on Staniel Cay with the finest catering and private chef services. Savor the flavors of paradise with NuKeitha Ferguson. Whether you're planning home dinners, parties, showers, wedding events, birthdays, or any special occasion, we've got you covered.

NuKeitha Ferguson Catering and Private Chef Services

With NuKeitha Ferguson Catering, you can enjoy gourmet meals crafted to perfection in the comfort of your own space. Their services include:

- **Private dinners.** Relish exquisite, personalized meals tailored to your taste.
- **Parties and showers.** Elevate your celebrations with their delectable catering options.
- **Wedding events.** Make your big day unforgettable with their bespoke wedding catering.
- **Birthdays and more.** Add a touch of elegance to your special occasions with their culinary expertise.

Freshly Baked Pastries to Delight Your Senses

Indulge in NuKeitha Ferguson's selection of freshly baked pastries, perfect for any time of day. Their attention to detail ensures that every bite is a moment to remember.

Contact NuKeitha Ferguson

Ready to experience the best culinary delights Staniel Cay offers? Call NuKeitha Ferguson Catering and Private Chef Services at 242-466-4365 to book your event.

Flyin' Pig Cafe

The Flyin' Pig Café serves an island-inspired breakfast, lunch, and dinner menu. They make every meal from scratch with fresh ingredients, sauces, and dressings made daily. You and your friends will fall in love with every bite. Get a taste of the island life and visit them today! They offer the island's only coffee shop and source the freshest coffee grounds and make every cup of coffee to order.

Do you have a special event that needs quality catering services in Staniel Cay? The Flyin' Pig also provides private dining services for you, your loved ones, or your special event. Their team is dedicated to creating a relaxing and enjoyable experience from the moment you walk in until you pay for your meal. Explore private dining options and book them for your next celebration in Staniel Cay.

Whether you're looking for the freshest food, want to wow your guests with authentic Bahamian dishes, check out the Flyin' Pig.

Airport Road at Embrace Resort

Phone: (242) 524-0951

Email: Info@embraceresort.com https://stanielcaycafe.com/

Dog's Bar and Grill on Staniel Cay

Dog's Bar and Grill is a hidden gem across the street from Staniel Cay Adventures, on the left side of the road, just past the village beach. The bar has a unique atmosphere that is both welcoming and fun, known as "the locals hang out" spot. If you're looking for traditional Bahamian fare, Big Dog's is the place for you. Located on left side of the road coming from the Yacht Club just after the Town Beach (across from Staniel Cay Adventures) , this casual restaurant offers dishes such as cracked conch, grilled lobster, and fish fingers and more. You can enjoy your meal in their small dining room or take it to-go and have a picnic on the beach. Their prices are reasonable, and the service is friendly. Open weekdays and Saturday from 10 am. to 10 pm.

Staniel Cay Yacht Club Restaurant

Staniel Cay Yacht Club Restaurant is one of the most popular dining destinations in the Exuma Cays. From fresh seafood to a delicious Bahamian inspired cuisine, this restaurant has it all. Whether you are a food enthusiast or just looking for a casual dining experience, the Staniel Cay Yacht Club Restaurant is a must-visit destination.

History of Staniel Cay Yacht Club Restaurant

The Staniel Cay Yacht Club Restaurant has a fascinating history. It all started in the 1950s when it was founded as a small marina with just a few slips. Over the years, the yacht club has become a global destination for yacht enthusiasts and travelers alike. Today, the yacht club boasts a world-class restaurant serving some of the Exuma Cays' most delicious dishes.

The Ambience and Atmosphere

The ambiance of Staniel Cay Yacht Club Restaurant is one of a kind. The restaurant is on the beach's edge, giving you a breathtaking water view. With its open-air design and island elegant décor, the restaurant is the perfect place to relax and enjoy a fine dining experience Bahamas style. The ambiance is ideal for a romantic dinner, family gathering, or meeting friends.

The Menu

The menu at Staniel Cay Yacht Club Restaurant is nothing short of impressive. You can expect to find a variety of fresh seafood, such as conch, lobster, and fish. You will also find international dishes such as steak and pasta. Their menu caters to everyone's tastes and preferences, so you can expect to find vegetarian options too. If you have special dietary needs, let them know when making your dinner reservation.

Signature Dishes

The menu at Staniel Cay Yacht Club Restaurant is diverse, so if you need help to decide what to order, try the signature dishes. The Lobster Quesadilla is one of the most popular dishes on the menu. They make it with succulent Bahamian lobster, grilled peppers, onions, and cheese, served with homemade salsa and guacamole. Another must-try dish is the Conch Fritters with a spicy dipping sauce.

Reservation and Service

Staniel Cay Yacht Club Restaurant is a hot spot for travelers, so it's recommended that you make lunch reservations in advance. Dinner reservations are a must, or you can dine off the lunch menu. Place your dinner order by 4:00 p.m. for one of two seatings. In SCYC tradition, the dinner bell rings for each seating. The restaurant is open for breakfast, lunch, and dinner, and the service is impeccable. Their staff is friendly, welcoming, and always willing to assist you. The restaurant also offers a takeout option so you can enjoy their delicious food at your own pace.

If you are looking for something cool and tropical, enjoy a frozen Mango Drink or a Pina colada.

The Staniel Cay Yacht Club Restaurant is a must-visit destination for travelers who want to experience the best of Bahamian cuisine. Everything about Staniel Cay Yacht Club Restaurant is exceptional, from its history to its signature dishes and welcoming atmosphere. Whether craving fresh seafood or trying something new, the restaurant's menu caters to everyone's taste buds. So, make a reservation today and get ready to indulge in a culinary adventure.

Staniel Cay Adventures and the Staniel Cay Yacht Club Lunch or Brunch in Paradise

Are you looking for the perfect day to soak up the sun and relax in a tropical paradise? Join the Staniel Cay Yacht Club and Staniel Cay Adventures for a private charter boat ride and lunch or brunch on a deserted beach or sandbar. They make paradise perfect.

As soon as you step aboard your private charter boat, the stresses of everyday life will melt away. Sailing through the turquoise waters of the Exuma Cays, you'll enjoy the sights of uninhabited islands and coves. But the highlight of your trip will be your lunch or brunch destination. They'll take you to a deserted beach or sandbar, where nothing but the sound of the waves and the sight of sand between your toes surrounds you. As you relax under an umbrella and sip drinks served by your private server, you'll feel like you're in your private paradise.

But they don't just offer relaxation; they also offer adventure. On your way back to Staniel Cay, they can stop to visit the Original Swimming Pigs if you'd like a unique and unforgettable experience. These friendly pigs will even swim out to greet you, hoping to receive a treat. Or, if you prefer, they can take you to snorkel at Thunderball Cave, where you'll feel like you're in a James Bond movie.

They'll cater to your every need with island-style décor and unsurpassed service. With only one seating available daily, you'll receive the personalized attention you deserve. Advanced dinner reservations are required so you can rest assured your adventure will be perfectly planned and executed.

If you're looking for an unforgettable experience in paradise, look no further than Staniel Cay, the Staniel Cay Yacht Club, and Staniel Cay Adventures. From a private boat ride through the Exuma Cays to a deserted beach or sandbar lunch or brunch, they can make your day perfect. With various beach games, swimming pigs, and snorkeling options, they offer relaxation and adventure. And with their unsurpassed service and island-style décor, you'll wish to take paradise home. Book your advanced reservation now, as there's only one seating per day, and spaces fill up quickly. Let them show you how they make a day in paradise perfect.

Contact info@StanielCayAdventures.com Text or Call (242) 524-8062 and WhatsApp

Da Bahamian Experience: A Bahamian Beach Adventure and Picnic

The Bahamas has rich culture, delicious food, and beautiful beaches. For travelers seeking to experience all the island paradise offers, Da Bahamian Experience provides the perfect day trip. With activities including fishing, grilling, and enjoying the white sandy beaches, this tour provides a unique and authentic look into the Bahamian way of life.

The best way to get to know a country is through its food. Therefore, Da Bahamian Experience starts with fishing. Guests can catch their own fish using traditional Bahamian techniques, such as handline fishing, spearfishing, and rod fishing. A guide will be on hand to teach and provide tips. Once you catch your fish, you can learn how to clean and prepare them with traditional Bahamian spices. This is a great way to get to know not just the food but also the culture of the Bahamas.

Conch is a staple in Bahamian cuisine, and Da Bahamian Experience allows guests to dive for their own conch. The captain will lead a group to dive for these large, spiral-shelled sea creatures, which are then cleaned and mixed with vegetables to create delicious and refreshing ceviche, called conch salad. Eating conch is a Bahamian tradition, and enjoying it with a beautiful beach view is the perfect way to enjoy it.

After all the activities, it's time to relax and enjoy the beauty of the Bahamas. The team at Da Bahamian Experience sets up a traditional beach grill on the white sandy beach where guests can enjoy the food they have prepared. The guide will demonstrate how to use the old-style grill while guests enjoy beach games, water towables, and traditional Bahamian music. This is a great way to spend the day soaking up the sun and enjoying all the Bahamas offer.

Da Bahamian Experience offers travelers a genuine look into Bahamian culture, traditions, and cuisine while enjoying all Paradise Island has beauty. Whether you are a seasoned traveler or this is your first time in the Bahamas, Da Bahamian Experience offers a unique and unforgettable experience you won't find on any other tour. The activities, food, and people make the Bahamas the perfect destination for those seeking adventure or relaxation. Book your trip now and experience the magic of the Bahamas firsthand!

Staniel Cay Adventures

info@StanielCayAdventures.com Text or Call (242) 524-8062 and WhatsApp

Discovering Paradise at McDuff's Restaurant on Norman's Cay

If you are looking for a picture-perfect tropical destination with crystal clear turquoise waters, white sandy beaches, and the freshest seafood, then Norman's Cay in the Bahamas is the place for you. Having the most famous hamburger in the Cays, it's my favorite day trip. Hire a guide, sit back, relax, and enjoy the incredible ride to Norman's Cays. There's no better place to indulge in fresh delicacies than McDuff's Restaurant on Norman's Cay. This beachfront restaurant offers a stunning view, a relaxed ambiance, and a menu that celebrates the flavors of the Bahamas.

The Atmosphere

You'll first notice the island vibe when entering McDuff's Restaurant. It's low-key and welcoming. The dining area is designed with a wooden deck and a thatched roof. The open-air establishment is decorated with hanging lights, wooden barstools, and colorful cushions that create a cozy and comforting feel.

McDuff's menu is simple, but everything on it is incredibly fresh and full of flavor. The restaurant's top-notch chefs prepare Bahamian dishes using locally caught seafood, meat, and vegetables. The menu includes appetizers such as conch fritters and cracked conch, which are two of the most famous Bahamian seafood dishes. For the main course, you'll find mouth-watering grilled lobster, grilled Mahi-Mahi, and a Bahamian take on the classic fish and chips.

The Drinks

If you're looking for tropical cocktails to accompany your meal, McDuff's Restaurant has got you covered. They stock their bar with local beers, wine, and innovative cocktails to fit all tastes. Their signature drink, Bull Shot, is a must-try. It's made with local rum, vodka, and a hint of guava nectar that gives it a unique island flavor. The bartenders are innovative in their creations and can whip up anything you desire while you take in the beautiful surroundings.

The Service

McDuff's staff is friendly, welcoming, and responsive. Their customer service is first class, making your dining experience even more special. The servers are knowledgeable about the menu and recommendations. They go above and beyond to ensure you are comfortable and satisfied with their dishes, including the quality of their service and attentiveness.

A Family-Friendly Environment

McDuff's is a family-friendly establishment that welcomes children of all ages. The restaurant provides a kid's menu with the same dishes as the adults, but in smaller portions. Children will love munching on macaroni and cheese or fish fingers while enjoying the sea breeze.

A visit to McDuff's Restaurant on Normans Cay is an experience you won't forget. This beachfront restaurant offers good food, drinks, unparalleled ocean views, excellent service and a comfortable atmosphere to dine in. It's a top-rated restaurant with something to offer everyone, whether you are with friends or family, or looking for a calm, serene getaway by yourself. Plan your next trip to the Bahamas and experience one of Normans Cay's hidden paradise.

http://macduffscottages.com/

NORMAN'S CAY, THE BAHAMAS +1 (844) 462.2383 +1 (242) 805.2235

Cottage Reservations: +1 (242)-357-9501

Restaurant Reservations +1 (242)-805-2235

Farmers Cay Yacht Club

Rent your own private island paradise for the day and enjoy a Bahamian cook out with Staniel Cay Yacht Club and Staniel Cay Adventures.

Are you searching for an exclusive and luxurious escape from the everyday hustle and bustle of your life? Look no further than a Private Island Experience based on the Bahamas. You'll experience the perfect blend of serenity, luxury, and privacy that's hard to find elsewhere. Their luxurious beachfront cabanas, accompanied by a bar, BBQ, mini-fridge, dining table, lounge chairs, umbrellas, Wi-Fi, and a Bluetooth speaker system, are the perfect way to unwind and recharge yourself. Moreover, they provide a unique chance to rent a private island paradise and indulge in a Bahamian cook out. Whether you're celebrating engagements, birthdays, weddings, anniversaries, or planning a private beach party, they have all you would ever want! So, why wait? Experience a perfect getaway today!

This small, private island with just a short boat ride from Staniel Cay. The island is surrounded by breathtaking natural beauty. As you bask in the sun, you'll witness the stunning blue waters and white sandy beaches. The island features a dock designed for boats up to 40 feet, a freshwater sink, and a shower. You'll find it incredibly convenient for your day trip needs.

They want you to have a stress-free and enjoyable day on their private island. They ensure you will have all your amenities, such as lounge chairs, umbrellas, and even Wi-Fi, to make your visit even more comfortable.

In addition to indulging in the beauty of our private island, you can book a Bahamian cook out to make your visit a truly unique experience. There's something about a barbeque that brings people together—and what better place to experience that than on a private island in the Bahamas?

info@StanielCayAdventures.com Text or Call (242) 524-8062 and What'sApp

Fowl Cay Resort Hill Top

Boaters and visitors to the surrounding islands are welcome to book dinner (reservation only) for hors d'oeuvres and cocktails from 6:30 p.m., with dinner seating 7:30 p.m. to 9:00 p.m. For dinner reservations, contact them at 242-557-3179 or VHF Channel 16. Please note you must provide transportation to the restaurant dock. Hire a boat captain from the location you are staying in. A local professional must navigate the waters at night as it is extremely dangerous.

Cocktail hour: **6:30 - 7:30 PM**

Seated dinner: **7:30 - 9:00 PM**

Restaurant: dinner@fowlcay.com

Check Out These Great Restaurants as Well

Emerald Sunset View in Black Point

Address: Great Guana Cay Black point Black point Exuma cays, Bahamas

Hours:

Open: Closes 11:30 PM

Phone: +1 242-355-3219

Deshamon Restaurant & Bar

Dine-in · Takeout From the government dock, turn right first restaurant on the left

Address: 3HWX+J86, Great Guana Cay, Black Point, Bahamas

Phone: +1 242-355-3122

Scorpios Inn Restaurant & bar

Service options: Dine-in · Takeout · No delivery They have their own dock.

Address: 3HWX+82F, Great Guana Cay, Black Point, Bahamas

Phone: +1 242-355-3003

Black Point Yacht Club & Cottages

Address: 3HWW+HP, Bahamas

Phone: +1 242-357-0606

Lorraine's café

Service options: Dine-in · Takeout · No delivery

Black Point Great Guana Cay, Bahamas

Phone: +1 242-355-3095

Ocean Cabin On Farmers Cay

Little Farmer's Cay, Bahamas

Phone: +1 242-355-4006

Whether you're in the mood for a fancy dinner or a casual beachside lunch, there are plenty of dining options on and around Staniel Cay. From traditional Bahamian dishes to international cuisine, you'll find something to tickle your taste buds. So, eat, drink, be merry, and create memories on this beautiful island that will last a lifetime.

Staniel Cay Unveiled

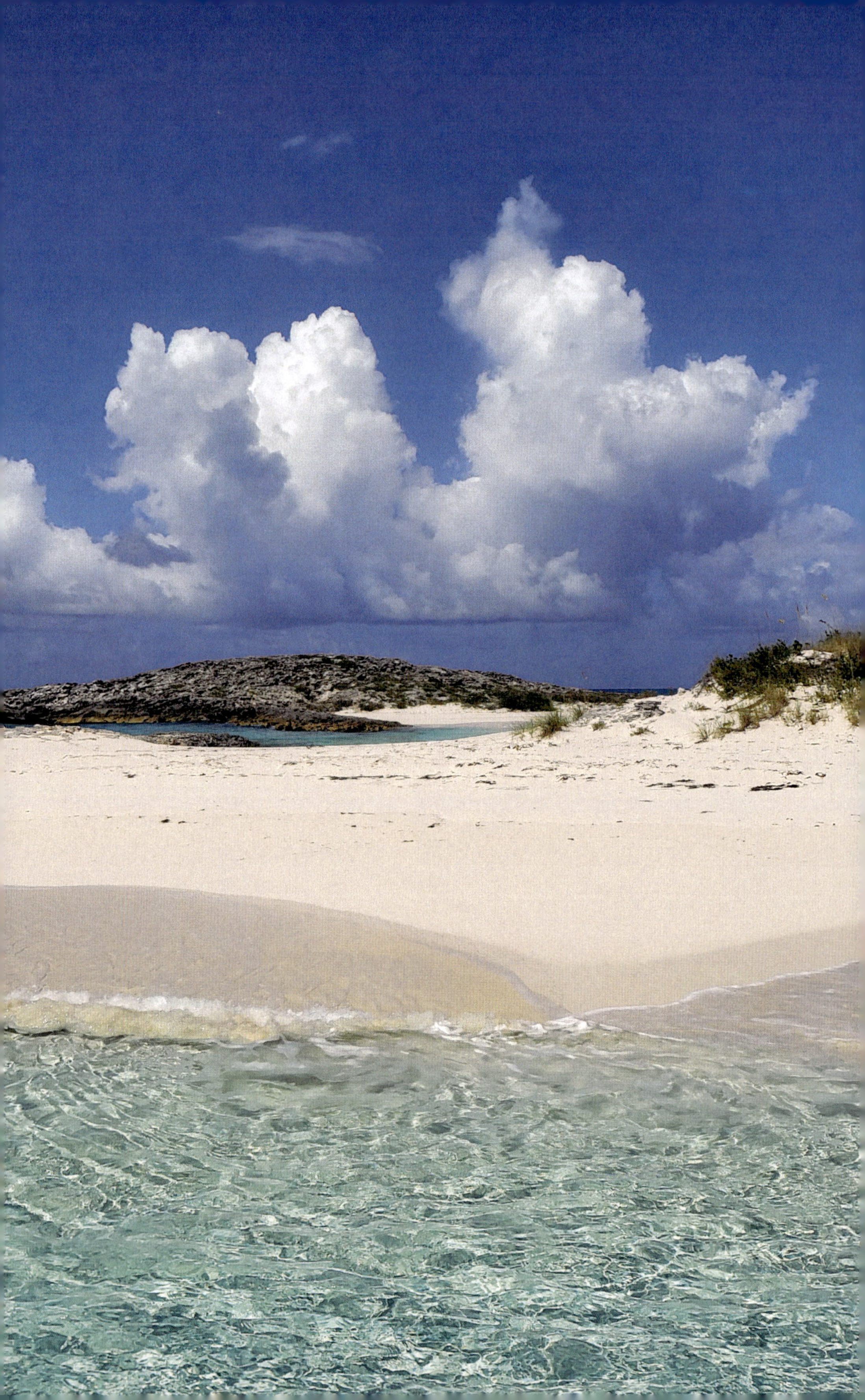

CHAPTER Eight

Experience the Beauty of Nature at Exuma Land and Sea Park in the Bahamas

Exuma Land and Sea Park

The Exuma Cays are a tapestry of stunning tropical islands extending over a kaleidoscope of azure blue and green waters. Known for their tranquil beauty, crystalline seas, and rich underwater wildlife, the Exuma Cays are a haven for travelers, sailors, and nature lovers alike. Among the jewels of the Exuma Cays is the Exuma Land and Sea Park, a pristine area protected from exploitation and brimming with adventures for the curious explorer.

The park is the first land and sea park in the world, covering around 176 square miles of land and sea. It is truly a magnificent place for exploring natural beauty, as its blue and turquoise waters, vast sandbanks, and secluded beaches house an array of interesting flora and fauna. This pristine paradise extends from Wax Cay Cut in the north to Conch Cut in the south, and up to four nautical miles on either side of the cays. It's a protected no-take zone, meaning you can remove nothing, living or dead, from the park. You'll find the headquarters and visitors' center on Warderick Wells, with several mooring sites scattered throughout the park. Get ready to explore the untouched beauty of Exuma Cays!

History of the Exuma Land and Sea Park

The Exuma Land and Sea Park (ELSP) is in the central-eastern part of the Bahamian archipelago, stretching from Wax Cay Cut to Conch Cut. The Bahamas National Trust (BNT) established the park in 1958, making it the world's first land and sea park. They manage the park and have designated it as a no-take zone, meaning, unless you have permission, you may not fish, swim, or anchor on the land or water surfaces within the park boundaries. Visit the Bahamas National Trust website, https://bnt.bs/explore/exuma/exuma-cays-land-sea-park/, for more information.

Key Attractions

- **Spectacular marine environment.** Prepare to be amazed by the dazzling array of sea life. With the park being a no-take zone, you'll encounter an undisturbed habitat rich in biodiversity.
- **Vibrant coral reefs.** Don your snorkeling or diving gear and immerse yourself in underwater worlds teeming with vibrant coral reefs bustling with parrotfish, angelfish, and even the occasional turtle or dolphin.
- **Pristine beaches.** The park boasts untouched sandy stretches, perfect for sunbathing, beachcombing, or simply basking in the serenity of a natural paradise.
- **Hiking trails.** For those looking to stretch their legs, scenic trails allow you to explore the various cays within the park and catch breathtaking panoramic views.

Activities

Snorkeling and diving. Exuma Land and Sea Park is an excellent place for snorkeling and scuba diving. Scuba diving and tank fills only available through Staniel Cay Adventures; 242.524.8062, Info@stanielcayadventures.com. The warm, clear waters are home to many species of marine life, including tropical fish, barracudas, turtles, sharks, and rays. The park has eighteen mooring sites where you can snorkel and see the creatures. Some popular snorkeling spots include the Eastern Shores, the Rocky Dundas, and the Aquarium, where you can observe some of the rarest marine life in their natural habitat.

The clear, calm waters make for exceptional conditions to explore the life under the waves. Specialized tours available from nearby islands offer guided excursions.

Kayaking and paddleboarding. Glide over the glassy surface of the Exuma Cays' waterways and navigate through mangrove environments alongside stunning coastlines.

Bird watching. The cays harbor a variety of bird species, making it a delightful spot for ornithology aficionados.

Photography. ELSP is a landscape photographer's dream, with dramatic sunsets, unspoiled beaches, and vibrant marine life offering countless opportunities to capture the essence of the Bahamas.

EXUMA CAYS LAND and SEA Park
Dinghy and Snorkeling Guide

Snorkeling offers every visitor the opportunity to enjoy the natural beauty of the park's underwater environment. This guide will help you safely locate prime snorkeling areas by dinghy.

Before you start your snorkeling adventure, read the following guidelines designed to protect this unique and beautiful environment and to protect you.

Respect Our Environment—Please Don't Damage the Coral

- **Look but don't disturb.** Coral reefs are hundreds of years old, built by very slow growing micro-organisms, and many of our reefs were in the Bahamas to welcome Columbus to the new world. **The damage you see today is caused by careless human contact.**

- Many of the reefs mentioned in this guide are very shallow, especially at low tide. These locations are included so their beauty may be enjoyed by every age group, but it is critical that you do not touch the coral, damage the reef with your outboard motor, kick it with your fins while swimming or stand on the coral to clear your mask.

- We have placed dinghy moorings at many of the locations indicated in our guide. Please use these moorings to avoid damaging the reefs with your anchor. It's OK for several dinghies to share the same mooring. If a dinghy mooring is unavailable, please anchor in sand a safe distance from the reef.

- You will also notice **bleaching and green algae** on much of the coral that is not constantly cleaned by tidal currents. Bleaching and algae growth are directly related to the warmer waters caused by global warming.

Snorkel Safely—Respect the Tide and Current

- Our most colorful reefs are cleaned twice a day by **strong tidal currents** and snorkeling these reefs is safest with minimal current at either low or high tide. Display a **dive flag** and always **keep one person in your dinghy** to watch the snorkelers and be ready to rescue anyone caught in the current.

- Inexperienced snorkelers may wish to swim with a flotation or use a glass bottom bucket from a dinghy to view underwater marine life.

- Use waterproof charts (available at the Ranger Station) to help locate the reefs and please take a working portable marine radio with you. Please notify "Exuma Park" on channel 16 if you encounter any problems.

You will see a wide variety of marine life on the reefs: coral, tropical fish, lobsters, sting rays, barracuda, and the occasional shark. Take photos (we have underwater cameras at the Ranger Station) and use our waterproof guides to help identify the marine life you see. Remember—no fishing, shelling, conching, or lobstering is permitted in the park. Please don't feed the fish!

Take Only Photographs—Leave Only Bubbles
Thank you for helping us preserve the natural beauty of The Bahamas.

Travel Tips

Access: You can access the park by boat. There are no facilities for overnight stays within the park itself, but nearby islands offer accommodation.

Unforgettable Boat Tours

Explore the wonders of ELSP effortlessly with a must-do boat tour. Discover remote areas of the park inaccessible by foot and learn about its intriguing history with a knowledgeable tour guide. Snorkel or scuba dive and witness the park's incredible marine life. Even if you take an all-day tour, you'll still be amazed at how much you didn't see. One area not to miss is the lazy river at Shroud Cay.

- **Best Time to Visit:** The Bahamas enjoy pleasant weather year-round, with the drier season between November and April being peak tourist season.

Conservation efforts. The park encourages visitors to support its conservation efforts by following all rules and guidelines, minimizing waste, and respecting wildlife.

Home to Abundant Wildlife

Besides marine life, the ELSP is a vital habitat for many bird species. Discover the magnificent seabirds that call the Exuma Cays home from April to August! Take a trip to Shroud Cay's eastern cliffs to witness a large colony of white-tailed tropicbirds, nesting clapper rails, and yellow warblers. Head over to Long Rock (aka Long Cay) to see the largest known nesting colony of Audubon's Shearwaters in the area—these nocturnal birds only come ashore at night. Warderick Wells boasts a breathtaking colony of white-tailed tropicbirds nesting on the seaward cliffs at the north end of the island, alongside least terns and Wilson's plovers. Other common resident birds include the Bahama mockingbird, black-faced grassquit, and osprey. Don't miss your chance to observe these beautiful birds, including gray kingbirds and Antillean nighthawks that call the Exuma Cays their summer homes. The park is even home to boa constrictors, iguanas, and the rare Bahamian hutia, which you can observe from a safe distance.

A Natural Oasis for Different Plant Species

The ELSP is a beautiful marine park and a natural oasis for different plant species. In the park, you can find many plants and trees that are rare or unique to the region. The Bahamian pine, silver top palm, and sea grapes are some of the most common plants found in the park. The vegetation comprises mangrove communities, with the east sides being clad in low scrub and the western sides with taller scrub. There are many epiphytic orchids and bromeliads. Take nature walks to explore the island's natural beauty and see the variety of plant species.

- **Safety:** Always be prepared when engaging in water activities. Utilize local guides and tour operators familiar with the tides, currents, and best spots to visit.

Shroud Cay: A Hidden Paradise in the Exuma Cays

If you're seeking tranquility and unparalleled beauty in the Bahamas, Shroud Cay is a destination you cannot miss. Nestled within the ELSP, this island is an untouched gem accessible only by boat. It offers a serene escape from the hustle and bustle of everyday life.

Why Shroud Cay is a Must-Experience

Shroud Cay is more than just a spot on the map; it's a sanctuary where nature thrives in its purest form. Whether you're a nature lover, an adventurous traveler, or simply someone in search of peace, Shroud Cay is your ideal retreat.

What Awaits You at Shroud Cay

- **Breathtaking landscapes.** Marvel at the stunning cays that make up this paradise. Each view is more beautiful than the last.
- **Exclusive access.** Reachable only by boat, Shroud Cay offers a secluded experience away from crowded tourist spots.
- **Natural serenity.** Allow your worries to melt away as you immerse yourself in the tranquil surroundings.

Perfect for Every Traveler

- **Nature enthusiasts** will find endless opportunities to explore diverse ecosystems.
- **Adventure seekers** can enjoy kayaking through mangrove creeks or snorkeling in crystal-clear waters.
- **Serenity seekers** will appreciate the peaceful atmosphere, perfect for relaxation and reflection.

This is an experience.

Awe-Inspiring Beach

Shroud Cay features a beautiful white sand beach surrounded by an expanse of lush mangrove vegetation. The beach is an ideal place to unwind and soak in some sun. The contrast between the white sand and the greenery is mesmerizing, and it's bound to leave you breathless. You can also go for a swim in the crystal-clear waters around the island. And the best part is that there is rarely anyone else around!

Camp Driftwood

Camp Driftwood sits on a hill overlooking the Shroud Cay beach. It's a quaint little spot made famous by a hermit who dug the steps to the top, leaving behind pieces of driftwood, to which people have added to ever since. The camp is a great place to take a break from the sun and relax in the shade. You'll also find amazing views of the island from the spot; it's perfect for taking pictures.

The Natural Whirlpool

The current around Camp Driftwood creates a natural whirlpool that spins you right onto the powdery beach. It's a thrilling ride that's bound to leave you laughing. The locals call it the washing machine, and it's a must-experience when you're on the island. It's safe for children and adults alike, and it's guaranteed to be a highlight of your trip.

Snorkeling

If you're an adventure-seeker, Shroud Cay has a lot to offer. The waters around the island are home to an array of marine life, including colorful fish and coral reefs. You can grab some snorkeling gear and explore the underwater world around the island. You don't need to be a pro to enjoy the experience; snorkeling is easy, and the waters around Shroud Cay are perfect for it.

Bird Watching

Shroud Cay is home to various species of birds, including pelicans, egrets, and herons. You'll also find several types of migratory birds on the island. If you're into birdwatching, Shroud Cay is a perfect spot to indulge in your hobby. Explore the hiking trails and spot some of the most beautiful birds you've ever seen.

A Peaceful Hiking Destination

Hiking is a great option for visitors who want to exercise and see the park's beauty close and personal. There are designated trails, including the Bitter Guana Trail, which take you through the park's wetlands and forests, and the breathtaking Sand Dollar Beach Trail. These hiking trails are relatively easy and suitable for people of all ages and fitness levels.

Shroud Cay is not just a destination; it's an experience that will leave you in awe. Plan your visit to this hidden paradise and discover the beauty of the Bahamas like never before.

The Shroud Cay in the ELSP is a perfect destination for travelers seeking a serene and untouched island experience. With its breathtaking beach, Camp Driftwood, the natural whirlpool, snorkeling, and bird watching, there's something for everyone. Remember to add the Shroud Cay to your itinerary for your trip to the Bahamas. It's a hidden gem that will leave you feeling refreshed and rejuvenated.

Little Pigeon Cay (Private)

Hawksbill Cay

Little Hawksbill Cay (Private)

Little Cistern Cay

Cistern Cay, also known as Indigo Island (Private)

Long Cay

Warderick Wells Cay (Park Headquarters)

Exploring the Heart of the Exuma Cays: Warderick Wells Cay

Nestled amid the sapphire waters of the Bahamas, Warderick Wells Cay offers an unspoiled oasis for travel enthusiasts, nature lovers, and eco-tourists alike. As the headquarters for the ELSP, this stunning island is a testament to the beauty of untouched nature and the importance of conservation.

A Pristine Paradise: Exuma Land and Sea Park

The ELSP, known for its rich biodiversity and vibrant marine life, is a sanctuary for researchers, divers, and those seeking a retreat from the trappings of modern life. Warderick Wells Cay, located at the center of this aquatic haven, serves as the perfect gateway to the park's wonders. With meticulously preserved coral reefs, mangroves, and beaches, the island encapsulates the soul of the Bahamas' environmental pride.

Journey Through an Untouched Land

The cay invites visitors on a journey through a mix of nature trails featuring the island's diverse landscape. The terrain offers everything from soft, sandy beaches to rugged rocky outcrops, providing a backdrop for some of nature's most breathtaking designs.

Hiking to the top of Boo Boo Hill, the cay's highest point, rewards adventurers with panoramic views of the surrounding cays and the vast expanse of the azure Caribbean Sea. The hill also sports "blowholes" where, with the right sea conditions, the waves rushing through the rock passages below create haunting moans.

Beneath the Waves: A Diver's Utopia

Diving enthusiasts will find Warderick Wells Cay particularly enchanting, with its crystal-clear waters offering visibility that can exceed an impressive hundred feet on a calm day. The no-take zone within the park has allowed for the marine life to flourish, including vibrant coral reefs and schools of fish playfully darting among the undersea topography.

Snorkelers, too, can explore the shallower waters where sea stars dot the sands and sea turtles often glide gently by, oblivious to their admirers above.

Mooring with Meaning

For those arriving by boat, the mooring system at Warderick Wells Cay is a sustainable approach to marine conservation. It minimizes anchor damage and helps preserve the coral gardens the park is dedicated to protecting. The cay offers several mooring buoys for overnight stays, where travelers can fall asleep to the gentle lapping of the waves and awaken to the unfiltered chorus of nature.

A Tapestry of Wildlife

On land, the island is home to a spectrum of wildlife, from curly-tailed lizards to the Bahamian hutia, a native rodent and the only land mammal of the Bahamas. Bird watchers will delight in the variety of avian species, such as the Bahama mockingbird and the red-legged thrush. Each animal plays a role in the delicate balance of this unique ecosystem, further emphasizing the importance of conservation efforts.

The Sustainable Traveler's Dream

Sustainability and responsible travel are at the heart of the visitor experience on Warderick Wells Cay. The park operates under principles that ensure minimal human impact, making it a haven for eco-tourists who wish to immerse themselves in nature without leaving a trace. With its solar-powered headquarters and commitment to protecting the marine environment, the ELSP is a pioneer in eco-tourism. Visitors are not just guests but become part of the cay's ongoing legacy of environmental stewardship.

Endless Memories Await

Whether you long for the serenity of sunsets casting a golden glow over quiet waters, or the adventure of exploring underwater treasures, Warderick Wells Cay in the ELSP offers a world where time seems to stand still and nature speaks most profoundly.

Plan your visit to Warderick Wells Cay today. Delve into the untouched beauty of the Bahamas, reconnect with nature, and embark on a trip that promises to leave a lasting imprint on your soul. Join the ranks of those who this extraordinary fragment of our planet has captivated and let the spirit of exploration lead the way.

White Bay Cay (Private)

Halls Pond Cay (Private)

Osprey Cay (Private, but landing permitted)

Little Halls Pond Cay (Private)

Soldier Cay (Private)

O'Briens Cay Discover the Untouched Beauty of O'Briens Cay in Exuma Land and Sea Park

Nestled in the heart of the Bahamian archipelago, within the ELSP, lies a hidden gem waiting to be discovered: O'Briens Cay. This idyllic spot is a slice of paradise that beckons travel enthusiasts, nature lovers, and adventure seekers alike. Let's explore the enchanting allure of O'Briens Cay and what makes it a must-visit destination on your next Caribbean adventure.

The Allure of O'Briens Cay A Sanctuary for Wildlife

O'Briens Cay is not just another picturesque island; it's part of the protected ELSP. This means the cay is a sanctuary for a wide array of marine life and terrestrial creatures. Travelers are encouraged to don their snorkels and fins to explore the underwater ballet of colorful fish and coral gardens that flourish here, safe from fishing and commercial activity.

An Adventure Seeker's Paradise

For those who crave adrenaline, O'Briens Cay delivers. Take part in thrilling water sports like kayaking, windsurfing, or stand-up paddleboarding through the crystalline waters. For divers, the surrounding reefs offer once-in-a-lifetime glimpses of the rich underwater biodiversity. And sailing enthusiasts will find this region perfect for catching the trade winds in their sails.

Tranquility Amid Natural Beauty

Travelers looking to unwind will appreciate the serene beaches and soft whispers of the waves. The powdery white sands are ideal for a day of sunbathing, while the scenic trails invite visitors for leisurely strolls or intimate picnics. Every moment on O'Briens Cay is an invitation to breathe deeply and simply be present amid the natural beauty.

Exuma Land and Sea Park

O'Briens Cay serves as a gateway to the wider ELSP. Spanning over 176 square miles of preserved land and sea, this park is a testament to the Bahamas' commitment to environmental conservation. The park bristles with life, where landscapes seamlessly transition from lush mangroves to deep blue depths, creating a sanctuary for both visitors and wildlife.

Planning Your Visit

When planning your trip to O'Briens Cay, consider staying at one of the charming eco-resorts or live-aboard vessels that dot the surrounding waters. This ensures your stay contributes to the preservation efforts of the park. Remember to pack eco-friendly sunscreen and respect all guidelines to minimize your impact on this pristine environment.

Lastly, be sure to check with local regulations and potential seasonal closures protecting the nesting sites of sea turtles and birds. This small effort on your part helps maintain the delicate balance of this exceptional ecosystem.

Conclusion: Embrace the Call of O'Briens Cay

At O'Briens Cay, every view is a postcard, every breath is a taste of purity, and every experience is a treasure. It is a place where the whispers of the ocean encourage you to let go of life's hustle and drift into the rhythm of island time. Embrace the call of the cay and let the tales of the winds and waves guide you to this enchanting nook of the Bahamas. O'Briens

Cay doesn't just promise an escape; it is an immersion into a world of tranquility, adventure, and awe-inspiring moments. So pack your bags, set your out-of-office email, and head out to where the blues of the sky and sea compete for your admiration. Whether you're a seasoned traveler or a greenhorn to the tropics, make your next journey one that leads to the unforgettable shores of O'Briens Cay, in the heart of Exuma's sanctuary of sea and sky. Adventures await at O'Briens Cay—an unspoiled canvas of natural wonders.

Pasture Cay (landing prohibited, critical iguana population)

Bell Island (Private)

Little Bells Cay/Cambridge Cay (Private, but landing permitted)

Rocky Dundas Discover the Majesty of Rocky Dundas: The Hidden Gem of Exuma Land and Sea Park

Nestled in the sapphire-blue canvas of the Bahamas, the Exuma Cays epitomize a tropical paradise. The isolated chain of islands boasts some of the most pristine ecosystems on the planet, with luminescent waters and abundant marine life that beckon the discerning traveler. For nature lovers, adventure seekers, and snorkeling enthusiasts alike, these islands offer an unparalleled opportunity to commune with nature's unspoiled beauty.

Introducing Rocky Dundas

Among the Exuma Cays, the Rocky Dundas Cay remains one of the most mesmerizing secrets, hidden within the heart of the ELSP. These twin limestone caverns rise majestically from the crystal-clear sea, their sun-dappled interiors home to stunning stalactites and native Bahamian cave paintings.

The Snorkeling Experience

Snorkeling around Rocky Dundas is an experience that belongs on every bucket list. Slip beneath the waves to explore the rich tapestry of life that thrives within the warm waters. As you navigate the colorful coral reefs, you'll witness a vibrant array of fish darting through the water, while graceful sea turtles might glide by as gentle ambassadors of the underwater realm.

Preserving Paradise

The ELSP is not just a place of exceptional beauty; it's also a pioneering effort in marine conservation. As you visit, remember you're a steward of this fragile environment. By respecting the guidelines set forth by conservationists, you help ensure that generations to come can enjoy the wonders of the Exumas.

Planning Your Visit

To fully experience Rocky Dundas, consider chartering a boat from one of the nearby islands or joining a guided tour to gain insight into this magnificent cay's geographical and cultural significance. As with any natural excursion, it's crucial to prepare adequately—bring sunscreen, ample water, and environmental awareness.

Supporting The ELSP

Nestled in the sapphire-blue waters of the Bahamas, the ELSP is a testament to nature's splendor and the need for its conscientious stewardship. As a marine protected area, the park has become a haven for a diverse range of wildlife and a beloved destination for eco-tourists, marine conservation enthusiasts, and travelers from across the globe. With its delicate ecosystems and the growing challenges faced by environmental conservation efforts, the park's vitality hinges upon the generous support of visitors like you.

Let's delve into how you can contribute to the continued success and preservation of this precious jewel. Your effort benefits the park and ensures a sustainable future for our marine life.

Become a Steward of Nature: Join the Support Fleet

By becoming a member of the ELSP Support Fleet, you are taking a significant step toward preserving an ecological treasure. A simple donation to the BNT grants you membership and the satisfaction of knowing your contribution aids the park's environmental and educational initiatives.

Partner in Conservation: Volunteer Your Time

Volunteerism forms the heartbeat of ELSP's operations. Lend a hand with ongoing projects by coordinating with the park office; even a few hours can make a lasting impact.

A Personal Commitment: Trash and Trail Maintenance

Every park visitor has the power to make a difference. Picking up ocean-borne trash during your exploration, maintaining trail markers, and following designated paths ensures we minimize our human footprint and protect the park's integrity.

Material Contributions: Fulfill a Wish

Before setting sail for the Exumas, consult the park's Wish List and consider bringing along essential items. Your spare parts or other supplies can significantly bolster the park's maintenance and operations.

Cash Donations: A Token for Rapid Action

Even modest cash donations can empower the park administrator with the flexibility to address immediate or unexpected needs. Contributing to the Friends of Exuma Park fund is an easy yet effective means of providing this vital support.

U.S. Citizens: Tax-Exempt Giving Through BEF

For United States citizens interested in contributing, the Bahamas Environmental Foundation (BEF), a registered 401-c3 organization, offers a tax-exempt route for your donation. By earmarking your funds for specific uses, you can directly influence the area of conservation that matters most to you.

Conclusion: Your Role in the Park's Legacy

The ELSP is more than a destination—it's a living classroom, a repository of biodiversity, and a blueprint for sustainable interaction with our world's precious marine environments. Whether through joining the Support Fleet, volunteering, contributing resources, or making a financial donation, your involvement has far-reaching implications. It's not just about preserving a strip of paradise; it's about safeguarding the future—one cay, coral, and creature at a time.

As we collectively navigate the waters of conservation, let us remember the ripple effect of each of our actions can grow into waves of positive change. So, as you plan your next adventure to the Bahamas, consider how you can contribute to the ELSP's enduring legacy. Your support is not just a gift to the park; it's an investment in a more conscientious and sustainable world.

Embrace the spirit of giving and chart a course toward conservation that will steer future generations toward a brighter, bluer tomorrow.

Conclusion

Rocky Dundas and the ELSP are more than just dots on a map; they represent a world where nature flourishes untouched, offering glimpses into Earth's primordial majesty. Whether you're peering into the deep from a boat deck or floating free in the embrace of the sea, hidden limestone caverns offer an experience both ethereal and profound. In the Exumas, each moment is an invitation to adventure, a call to explore, and a chance to witness the raw power and beauty of our planet. Come discover the untamed grandeur of Rocky Dundas—it's an encounter that will leave you transfixed and transformed.

Pack your fins, your sense of wonder, and journey to the heart of one of the Bahamas' most remarkable natural treasures. The Rocky Dundas is waiting to reveal all its hidden wonders. Are you ready to answer the call of the wild?

The ELSP is an emblem of natural wonder within the Exuma Cays, a place where the earth's raw beauty is on full display. Whether you're there for exhilarating aquatic adventures or soothing moments of seashore solitude, this amazing marine preserve stands as a testament to the value of conservation and the sheer delight of discovery. If pristine nature and engaging outdoor activities are what you seek, make sure the ELSP is on your travel itinerary.

Want to learn the history of the park and much more?

We recommend *The Exuma Park: What & How*, which has since become the most trusted resource for cruisers visiting the ELSP. Newly updated in 2023, this essential addition to your onboard library contains all the latest information regarding mooring and anchoring, activities, user fees, and ELSP regulations.

Written by (former) Senior Park Warden Brent Burrows II, this book explores the "what and how" of the ELSP and has tips for both first-time and seasoned cruisers alike. This Bahamas travel guide will provide all park guests with an inside look into the ELSP—supplying them with the information necessary to make their time spent visiting the park a magical and unforgettable experience. If you're planning a trip to the ELSP; the level of insight and advice given in this book can't be found elsewhere. You're sure to appreciate the tips and secrets from the Warden himself!

Be sure to purchase a copy and bring it with you during your preparation and cruising as you take part in the trip of a lifetime, exploring an incredibly pristine and beautiful area in every single way. The up-to-date information in this Exuma travel guide covers topics such as park operations, park regulations, trip planning, mooring and anchoring, user fees and payments, activities, and more. From Shroud Cay in the north, to Park Headquarters at Warderick Wells, to Cambridge Cay in the South—this must-have Bahamas cruising guide covers all the major Exuma Park islands and cays extensively.

Park Office Hours

Open: Mon–Fri 9am–5pm | Sun 9am–12pm
Contact: VHF - 09
24/7 emergency line: VHF - 16

VHF: Call "Exuma Park" on Channel # 09.

Channel #16 is monitored 24 hours a day for emergencies.

Coordinates of Exuma Cays Land and Sea Park Boundaries in Degrees / Minutes / Seconds

NW corner: Lat 24 deg 30' 37 " N Long 76 deg 52' 37"W | NE corner: Lat 24 deg 35' 30" N Long 76 deg 45' 50" W
SW corner: Lat 24 deg 14' 25" N Long 76 deg 36' 02" W | SE corner: Lat 24 deg 18' 37" N Long 76 deg 28' 47" W

Visit the ELSP website

https://bnt.bs/explore/exuma/exuma-cays-land-sea-park/

How To Report Poaching

Park Warden

Park Wardens request all visitors to report any poaching or other unusual activity they may observe—no fishing, shelling, conching of any kind is permitted within Exuma Park boundaries.

Call "Exuma Park" on Channel # 09 to report suspicious activity.

You can remain anonymous if desired—simply identify your vessel as "Miss Molly" or any other fictitious name to remain anonymous.

Bahamas Defence Force

The Bahamas Defence Force has stationed three officers at Park Headquarters to assist Park Staff with enforcement matters. Defence Force vessels frequently overnight at Park Headquarters as well.

Contact Defence Force on VHF #16

Exuma Cays Land and Sea Park
SEA AQUARIUM
Snorkel Site $12 per person

CHAPTER Nine

VISITING BLACK POINT ON GREAT GUANA CAY

Discover the Hidden Gem of Black Point, Great Guana Cay, Exuma, Bahamas

Why Visit Black Point?

Nestled in the heart of the Exuma chain, Black Point on Great Guana Cay is a hidden gem waiting for you to discover it. Known for its pristine beaches, vibrant local culture, and crystal-clear waters, this destination is a haven for travel enthusiasts, beach lovers, and fishing fans. Black Point is a retreat perfect for travelers who want to escape the hustle and bustle of city life. If you're yearning for an authentic Bahamian experience far from the crowded tourist spots, Black Point is the place to be. In this chapter, we'll explore this hidden paradise and give tips on what to do when visiting Black Point.

Getting to Black Point

Black Point is a quaint village on the island of Guana Cay, and it's easily accessible by boat or air from Staniel Cay or Nassau. The journey to Black Point is a beautiful experience in itself as you travel across the pristine crystal blue waters that the Bahamas is famous for. The boat ride takes around three hours from Nassau, two hours from Great Exuma, and fifteen minutes from Staniel Cay. Once you arrive, friendly locals who are happy to help you settle in the area will greet you.

Exploring Black Point

Black Point is a small village with fewer than five hundred people. The village's main attraction is the stunning powder soft beaches and clear waters surrounding it, making it an excellent spot for water activities. Some top things to do in Black Point include snorkeling, paddleboarding, kayaking, heading to incredible beaches, fishing, and enjoying the locals.

Marveling at the Black Point Blowhole

Many know the Bahamas for its numerous idyllic islands, coral reefs, and clear turquoise waters. Beyond those stunning attractions, the Bahamas also presents natural phenomena that are both intriguing and exciting. One such phenomenon is the blowhole at Black Point. The Black Point Blowhole is a natural wonder that amazes any traveler. It has unique features and is a must-see attraction in the Exuma Cays.

Located on the Atlantic side of the island, the Black Point Blowhole is a natural marine geyser that a combination of incoming waves and sea caves produces. When incoming waves get trapped in the sea caves, they create a hydraulic compression that forces the water through the opening in the cave ceiling. The result is an awe-inspiring sight where the ground trembles like an earthquake, and water shoots high in the sky through a hole in the rocks. It truly is an incredible experience that leaves any onlooker mesmerized. The best time to enjoy the Black Point Blowhole is during high tide and when there is a strong east or north-east wind. Those conditions enhance the power and force of the water, creating a more magnificent spectacle. Locals recommend travelers visit during that period to truly appreciate the full beauty of the Black Point Blowhole.

Standing next to the Black Point Blowhole is a unique experience that visitors must not miss. The sheer power of the water is overwhelming, and one can feel the energy generated beneath their feet. The sound of the water crashing against the rocks and the spray that emanates from the blowhole allow sightseers to appreciate its full beauty. Beautiful scenery that comprises sandy beaches, rugged coastlines, and lush foliage surrounds the Black Point Blowhole. After witnessing the blowhole, you can stroll along the beach, watch the local fishers in action, or enjoy seabirds soaring through the sky. It is a perfect spot to escape the hustle and bustle of city life and immerse yourself in nature's beauty.

In conclusion, the Black Point Blowhole is a natural wonder that is a must-visit for any traveler. It is a natural phenomenon that is both intriguing and awe-inspiring. Located in a beautiful part of the Bahamas, the Black Point Blowhole offers an unforgettable experience. The sheer power of the water, combined with the beautiful surroundings, is an experience that one must witness to fully appreciate. If you're planning a trip to the Bahamas, ensure you add the Black Point Blowhole to your itinerary and treat yourself to an experience that will leave you marveling for years to come.

Black Point, Bahamas: The Art of Platting

The ladies of Black Point are renowned for their intricate palm weaving. The small yet vibrant community has mastered transforming humble palm fronds into stunning works of art, from baskets and purses to other unique creations. Their handmade crafts have served practical purposes for centuries and become a symbol of cultural heritage and local pride.

The Legacy of Platting

Platting in Black Point isn't just a craft; it's a time-honored tradition passed down through generations. The skill and artistry involved in creating each piece are a testament to the dedication and craftsmanship of the artisans. Each item tells a story woven with care and rich in history.

Platting in Black Point begins with meticulously selecting the finest palm fronds. Artisans choose leaves that are supple yet strong, ensuring durability and flexibility. They then treat and prepare the fronds for the intricate weaving process, where expert hands transform them into beautiful, functional pieces.

The Process of Platting

Step 1: Harvesting and Preparing the Palms

> The process starts with harvesting young, green palm fronds, stripped of their outer layers and dried. That ensures the fibers are pliable and ready for weaving.

Step 2: Designing the Pattern

> Artisans often begin with a mental blueprint or sketch of the design, considering the pattern and purpose of the final product. Whether it's a basket for carrying fruits, or a purse for an elegant evening out, they carefully plan each item.

Step 3: Platting the Magic

> The actual weaving process requires skill and patience. Artisans use age-old techniques, weaving the strands over and under, creating intricate patterns and sturdy structures. Depending on the complexity of the design, that stage can take anywhere from a few hours to several days.

Step 4: From Black Point to Nassau

> While Black Point remains the heart of the craft, locals transport the beautifully woven plat works to Nassau, the capital of the Bahamas. In bustling markets and quaint boutiques, both locals and tourists alike

cherish the items. Visitors to Nassau can bring home a piece of Bahamian heritage, with each palm-woven product created using the Plat work from Black Point serving as a reminder of the craftsmanship and cultural richness of Black Point.

Supporting Local Artisans

Purchasing palm-woven products supports the Black Point artisans and helps preserve an invaluable tradition. By investing in handcrafted items, you're not just buying a unique souvenir—you're contributing to the livelihood of local families and the continuation of a cultural legacy.

The artistry of platting in Black Point, Bahamas, is more than just a skill; it's a vibrant expression of cultural identity and a testament to human creativity. For artisans and visitors alike, these woven treasures represent a deep connection between the land and the community. Whether you're an artisan looking to hone a new craft or a visitor eager to experience Bahamian culture, Black Point palm weavings can offer a unique and enriching experience.

For more information on exploring this art form or purchasing a piece of Black Point's legacy, visit Black Point and ask any locals who to see.

Food and Accommodation

There are several options available for food and accommodation in Black Point, ranging from high-end resorts to budget-friendly guesthouses. The Black Point Inn is one of the top-rated options in the area, with comfortable rooms, excellent food, and great views of the sea. You can also rent a private villa or a cozy beach hut for a more secluded experience. The resort offers various dining options, from seafood to local Bahamian cuisine, and all meals are cooked fresh using locally sourced ingredients.

Restaurants:

From traditional Bahamian cuisine to fresh seafood, the local restaurants in Black Point will tantalize your taste buds. Don't miss out on the conch salad, grilled fish, and other local specialties.

- Adderley's Rooms 242-355-3016.
- Long Bay Cottages 242-355-3064 / 3095; lorrainrolle@yahoo.com. Operated by Lorraine Rolle, offers two rental cottages.
- Black Point Vacation Rental Cottages; 242-355-3055. Terrance & Ida Patton offer cottages for rent overlooking the bay that sleep 2 to 4.

Black Point Yacht Club; 242-355-3003. https://blackpointexuma.com/ 242.524.0330

   info@blackpointexuma.com
- Susan's Bonefish Lodge; 242-355-3116 / 3010. Rooms and apartments.

Where to Shop for Groceries

You can find what you need even on a remote island like Black Point. The island has small grocery stores that stock essential items, fresh produce, and local delicacies. Make sure to try some native Bahamian treats.

Grocery: These stores are across the street from each other.

Adderley's Friendly Store 242-355-3016

J&D Convenience Store +1 242-355-3122 Attached to DeShamon's Restaurant.

Corene's Bread. DeShamon's Restaurant; order in the afternoon for a delivery the next day at noon—choices: cinnamon, raisin, whole wheat, coconut, and white breads.

Best bread ever made can be ordered from Lorraine's Café 242-355-3064 / 3095

Liquor Stores:

You can buy liquor from Lorraine's Café or Scorpio's https://blackpointexuma.com/.

Rent bicycles or **Golf Carts** Lorraine's Cafe 242-355-3064 / 3095; or Ida at the Laundry 242-355-3113

Boat Rental / Charter

Ocean Breeze Boat Rental Tour and Charter Service; 242-355-3070; 242-464-1181. Raymond Andrews offers a 23' Contender, a Boston Whaler, and four jet skis.

Villas and Boat Rentals (242) 524-8781; vacation@exumavacation.com.

Lorraine's Cafe; 242-355-3095. Offers 2 boats for rental; a Boston Whaler and a Nautica RIB.

Laundry Services

Traveling light? No problem. Black Point has laundry services available to ensure you always have fresh clothes, allowing you to pack light and focus on enjoying your trip.

Rockside Laundry Black Point

242-355-3113

rocksideinn@yahoo.com

Ida Patton. Ten washers and ten dryers.

https://www.facebook.com/Rockside-Laundramat-111747226863000/.

Churches

For those seeking a spiritual connection, Black Point offers a few charming churches where you can attend services and experience the island's strong community.

- Bible Mission Church
- Gethsemene Baptist
- St. Luke's Baptist

Fuel
- The closest source of fuel is the Staniel Cay Yacht Club

Things to Do

Relax on Stunning Beaches

> Black Point boasts some of the most beautiful beaches in the Bahamas. Picture yourself lounging on soft, white sand, surrounded by turquoise waters. Don't miss out on visiting the secluded coves and hidden bays that offer a perfect escape from the world.

Enjoy Water Activities

> The waters around Black Point are perfect for snorkeling, swimming, and kayaking. Adventure seekers can explore vibrant coral reefs teeming with marine life or paddle through serene mangrove forests.

Fishing Expeditions

> Black Point is a dream come true for fishers. Whether you're into deep-sea fishing or prefer casting a line from the shore, the abundance of fish species will keep you hooked.

Explore Local Culture

> Immerse yourself in the local Bahamian culture. Visit the island's historical landmarks, engage with the friendly locals, and experience the unique traditions and customs that make Black Point special.

Ready to explore the untouched beauty of Black Point, Guana Cay? It may be lesser known than some of the more famous Exuma Cays, but that's part of what makes it a hidden gem. The stunning beaches, clear waters, and friendly locals make it an ideal destination for travelers who want to experience a laid-back island lifestyle without the crowds. Black Point has something for everyone. So, pack your bags, and get ready for an unforgettable island adventure in one of the world's most beautiful destinations! Whether you're basking on the beach, exploring underwater worlds, or savoring local flavors, Black Point promises an experience like no other.

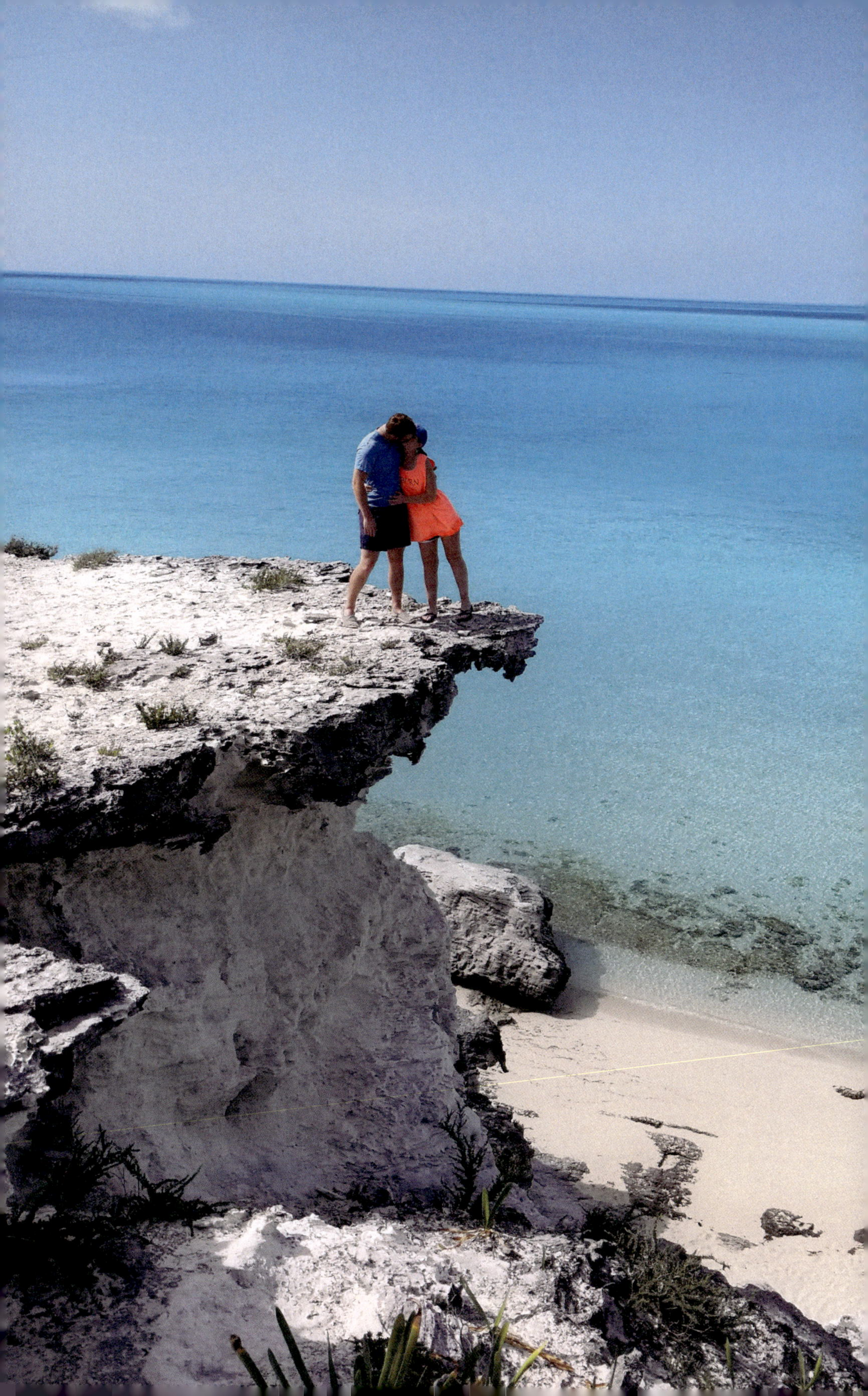

CHAPTER

Ten

Create Memories to Last a Lifetime at Fowl Cay Resort in the Exuma Cays

Are you tired of the same old vacation spots and looking for a unique adventure? Look no further than Fowl Cay Resort in the Exuma Cays! This private island resort is jam-packed with all-inclusive features, leaving you feeling truly pampered. Whether you're a thrill-seeker, water sports enthusiast, or simply looking to relax in paradise, Fowl Cay Resort has you covered.

Fowl Cay Resort is in the heart of the stunning Exuma Cays, an archipelago of 365 islands and cays. The resort is on a private island, guaranteeing seclusion and privacy that is scarce in other vacation destinations. And once you arrive, you'll quickly find they have everything you need for an incredible vacation experience.

One of the most exciting aspects of staying at Fowl Cay is that all guests receive a private boat for their stay. This means you'll be free to explore the Exuma Cays at your own pace, hopping from one island to the next, discovering all the gems the area offers, and making unforgettable memories.

Fishing enthusiasts will also be pleased to know Fowl Cay offers top-of-the-line fishing gear. Whether a seasoned pro or a beginner, you can fish for many species, including bonefish, barracuda, and snapper. And when you're done, you can even have your catch cooked up for dinner by the resort's talented chefs.

And the fun continues. Fowl Cay also offers a variety of watersport equipment, such as kayaks, paddleboards, and snorkeling gear. This means you can spend your days exploring the crystal-clear waters surrounding the resort and getting close and personal with the sea life that calls the Exuma Cays home.

If you're feeling hungry after all your excitement, don't worry—Fowl Cay has you covered with limitless food and drinks. The resort features a fully stocked oceanfront villa with a kitchen and bar. And you won't have to worry about cooking, either—the resort's skilled culinary team will prepare all your meals for you.

Fowl Cay Resort in the Exuma Cays is the perfect vacation destination for those looking to create memories that will last a lifetime. With a private powerboat, fishing gear, water sports equipment, and limitless food and drinks, this all-inclusive resort offers everything you need for the ultimate adventure experience.

Fowl Cay Resort Fowl Cay, Exuma

Book a villa (USA): 877-845-5275

Worldwide: 1-305-284-1300

Dinner reservations: 242-557-3179

Resort: info@fowlcay.com

Restaurant: dinner@fowlcay.com

VHF Channel 16

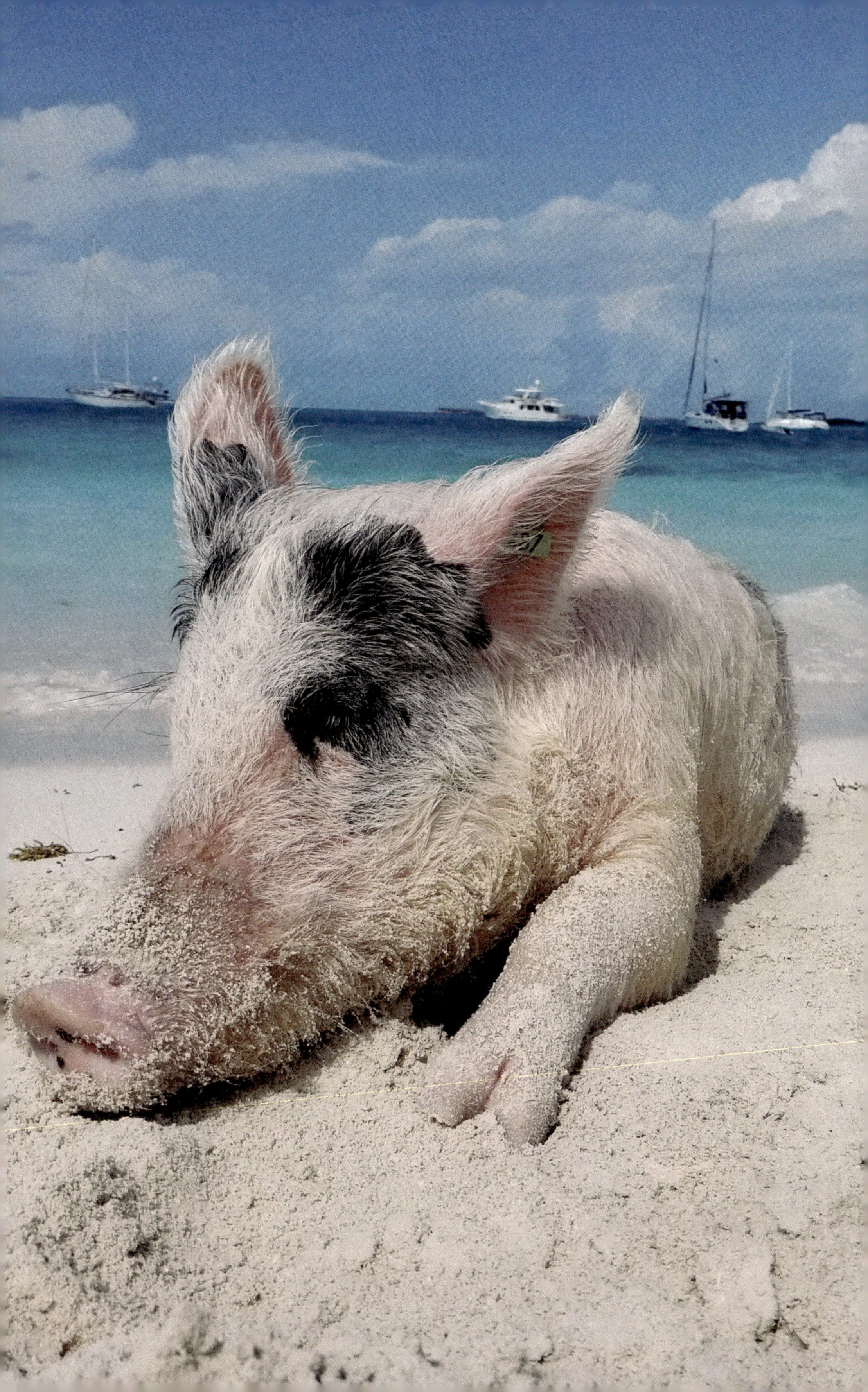

CHAPTER Eleven

LITTLE FARMERS CAY—A HAVEN FOR TURTLES

One island in the Exuma Cays that you should not miss is Little Farmers Cay, a small island between Great Exuma and Guana Cay Black Point. It's a rural island where you can experience an authentic Bahamian lifestyle and it's home to the friendliest turtles you will ever meet.

Little Farmers Cay is a haven for turtles, and the best part is that you can get up close and personal with them. The turtles in Little Farmers Cay are accustomed to humans, and they have no qualms about swimming along with you or eating out of your hand. Whether you're a seasoned snorkeler or a beginner, swimming with these gentle creatures is an unforgettable experience.

When you arrive in Little Farmers Cay, there are several ways to enjoy the turtles. You can swim with them in the shallow waters close to the shore, or if you are feeling adventurous, you can take a boat tour to the nearby turtle grass beds. The turtle grass beds are where turtles congregate to eat and play; you can see them in their natural habitat. If you're not a strong swimmer, don't worry because there are life vests available, and the water is shallow enough to stand in.

Apart from swimming with the turtles, there are other activities Little Farmers Cay offers. You can rent a bicycle and explore the island's quaint villages, visit the local museum to learn about the island's history, or sample some of the best Bahamian cuisine in the local restaurants. You can also take a boat tour to nearby cays and islands, such as Great Guana Cay, where you can hike to the island's famous sandbar, or Staniel Cay, where you can visit the famous swimming pigs.

One of the best times to visit Little Farmers Cay is during the annual Farmers Cay Regatta in late April or early May. The regatta is a week-long celebration of Bahamian culture, and it features boat races, dance performances, and a variety of food and drinks. It's a perfect opportunity to immerse yourself in the local community and witness the island's unique traditions.

Discovering Farmers Cay: A Hidden Gem in the Exuma Cays

While locations like Great Exuma and Staniel Cay often steal the spotlight, there's a lesser-known gem that offers an equally enchanting experience: Farmers Cay. Nestled in the heart of the Exuma Cays, Farmers Cay is a paradise for beach enthusiasts, travel bloggers, eco-tourists, and travelers seeking an off-the-beaten-path adventure.

The Allure of Farmers Cay

Farmers Cay is a small island with a big heart. Spanning just 360 acres, it may be diminutive, but it boasts a rich tapestry of natural beauty and cultural heritage. The island is home to a close-knit community that warmly welcomes visitors, making it a perfect destination for those looking to experience authentic Bahamian hospitality.

Pristine Beaches and Turquoise Waters

For beach enthusiasts, Farmers Cay is a dream come true. Powdery white sand beaches that stretch into the horizon adorn the island's coastline. The turquoise waters are not only visually stunning but perfect for swimming, snorkeling, and kayaking. One of the most popular spots is Little Farmers Cay Beach, where the calm, shallow waters are ideal for families and novice swimmers.

Unique Marine Life and Snorkeling Adventures

The underwater world around Farmers Cay is a treasure trove for snorkelers and divers and the surrounding coral reefs are teeming with vibrant marine life, including colorful fish, sea turtles, and even the occasional nurse shark. The famous Thunderball Grotto, a nearby underwater cave system, offers an unforgettable snorkeling experience. Named after the James Bond film *Thunderball*, this grotto is a must-visit for any adventure seeker.

Eco-Tourism Opportunities

Eco-tourists will find plenty to love about Farmers Cay. The island's commitment to sustainability and conservation is evident in its protected marine areas and eco-friendly practices. Guided eco-tours offer visitors the chance to explore the island's natural beauty while learning about its unique ecosystem. From mangrove forests to bird-watching excursions, there's no shortage of eco-adventures to embark on.

Cultural Experiences and Local Cuisine

One of the most enriching aspects of visiting Farmers Cay is the opportunity to immerse yourself in the local culture. The island hosts several festivals and events throughout the year, including the annual Farmers Cay Festival, which features traditional music, dance, and Bahamian cuisine.

The Farmers Cay Yacht Club

A visit to Farmers Cay wouldn't be complete without stopping by the Farmers Cay Yacht Club. This iconic establishment offers a taste of local life and serves as a hub for socializing and entertainment. Enjoy a meal at the restaurant, which serves up delicious Bahamian dishes made from fresh, locally sourced ingredients. Don't miss out on the conch fritters and grilled lobster, both island specialties.

Engaging with the Local Community

The residents of Farmers Cay are known for their warmth and hospitality. Engaging with the local community provides a deeper understanding of the island's history and traditions. Take a stroll through the village, visit local markets, and chat with the islanders to learn about their way of life. You might even hear fascinating stories about the island's past and its role in the larger history of the Bahamas.

How to Get There

Farmers Cay is accessible by boat or small aircraft. Many visitors choose to arrive by private yacht or charter a boat from Great Exuma or Nassau. The Farmers Cay Airport also accommodates small planes, making it a convenient option for those looking to fly in. Once on the island, getting around is easy, with golf carts and bicycles available for rent.

Accommodations on Farmers Cay

While Farmers Cay may not have large resorts found on other islands, it offers charming accommodations that provide an intimate experience. Guesthouses and vacation rentals are the primary options, each offering stunning views and easy access to the island's attractions. Staying on Farmers Cay allows visitors to fully immerse themselves in the island's tranquil ambiance.

Tips for Travelers

- **Plan ahead.** While Farmers Cay is a laid-back destination, it's essential to plan your trip in advance, especially if you're visiting during the peak season or festival times. Accommodations can fill up quickly, so booking early ensures you have a place to stay.
- **Pack light.** The island's casual atmosphere means you won't need to bring much. Lightweight clothing, swimwear, and comfortable footwear are all you need to enjoy your stay. Don't forget sunscreen and a hat to protect yourself from the sun.
- **Respect the environment.** Farmers Cay's natural beauty is one of its greatest assets. Help preserve it by practicing responsible tourism. Avoid leaving trash behind, respect wildlife, and adhere to local guidelines for environmental protection.
- **Engage respectfully.** When interacting with locals, be respectful and open-minded. Learning a few basic phrases in Bahamian Creole can go a long way in building rapport and showing appreciation for the local culture.

Conclusion

Little Farmers Cay Should Be Your Next Destination

Pristine Beaches

The beaches are immaculate, offering soft, white sand and tranquil turquoise waters. Whether you want to relax under the sun or take a refreshing dip, the beaches of Little Farmers Cay are perfect for both.

Vibrant Marine Life

Little Farmers Cay is home to an array of vibrant marine life. Snorkel or dive into the clear waters to discover colorful coral reefs, exotic fish, and, of course, friendly turtles. The underwater world is like no other, providing endless opportunities for exploration and adventure.

Rich Cultural Heritage

Experience the authentic Bahamian culture in its purest form. The residents of Little Farmers Cay are welcoming and eager to share their traditions and way of life. From local cuisine to traditional crafts, there's so much to learn and enjoy.

Perfect for Every Traveler

Whether you're a beach enthusiast, travel blogger, eco-tourist, or simply a traveler seeking a serene escape, Little Farmers Cay offers something for everyone. If you're planning to visit the Exuma Cays, make sure Little Farmers Cay is on your itinerary. This idyllic island offers an experience you'll treasure forever. Imagine swimming with turtles in crystal-clear waters, surrounded by breathtaking natural beauty. It's a place where you can disconnect from the hustle and bustle of everyday life and immerse yourself in natural beauty and cultural richness.

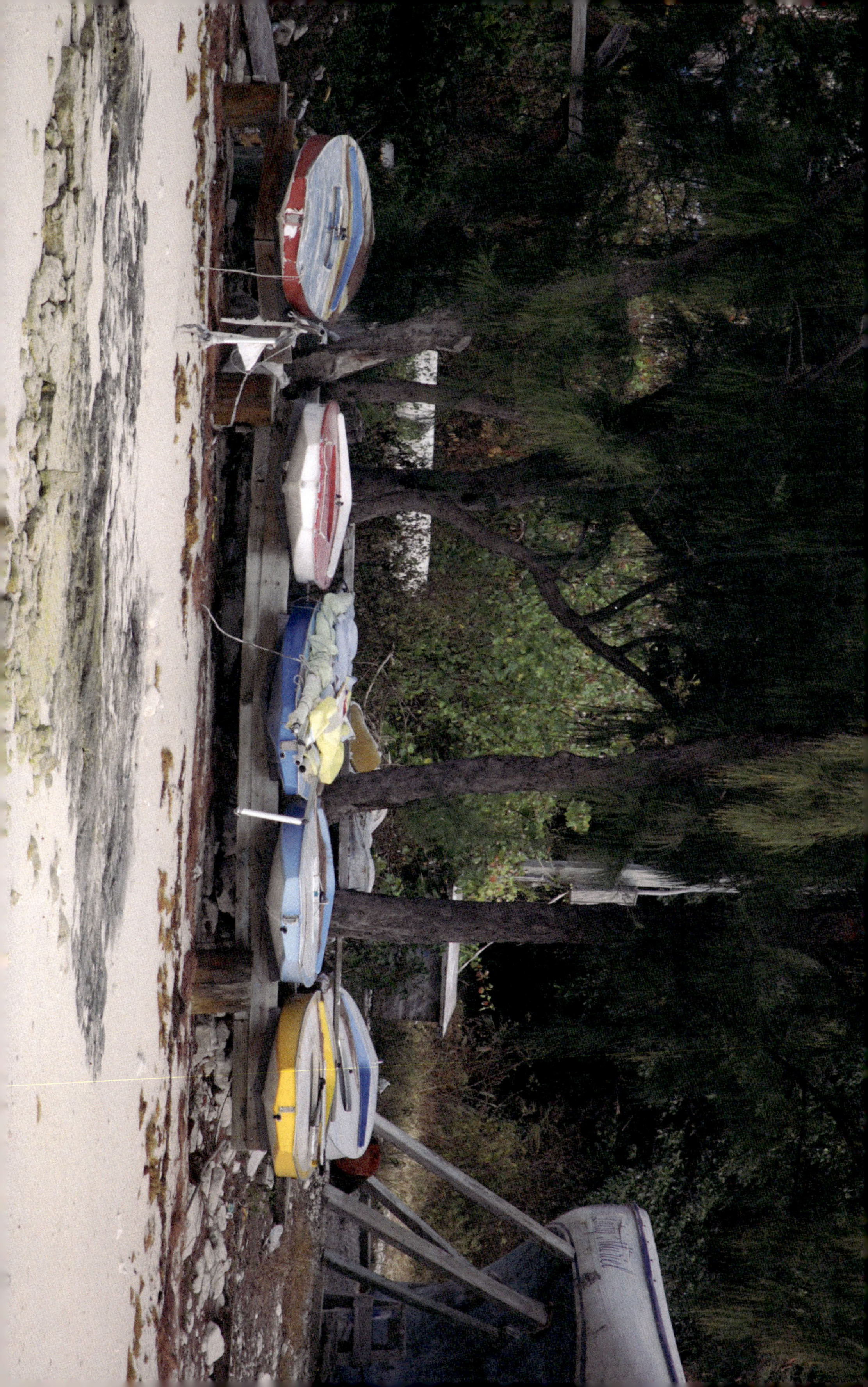

CHAPTER Twelve

Exploring Compass Cay in the Exuma Cays

Compass Cay in the Exuma Cays is one of the most unique islands in the Bahamas. Known for its serene beaches, crystal-clear waters, and famously friendly nurse sharks, Compass Cay is the perfect destination for those looking for an adventure-filled and quiet vacation. The island boasts a marina and is home to various wildlife, including turtles, iguanas, and the famous pet sharks! Compass Cay is not to be missed if you're planning a trip to the Exuma Cays and want to visit a destination like no other.

How to Get to Compass Cay in the Exuma Cays

Compass Cay is located in the Exuma Cays. To get there, you can take a flight to Nassau and then a connecting flight to Staniel Cay. From there, it's just a short a boat ride to Compass Cay. You can fly MakersAir to Staniel Cay from the USA and a boat to Compass Cay.

Exploring the Marina and Interacting with Sharks

Compass Cay is famous for its marina, which accommodates up to forty boats. The marina is well-equipped with floating docks, power and water services, and a fuel dock. The island also boasts several comfortable accommodations and amenities, such as a small snack and gift shop.

However, the main attraction of Compass Cay is undoubtedly the chance to interact with the local nurse sharks in the surrounding waters. The sharks are extremely friendly and will often approach swimmers and snorkelers. Though they're not harmful, visitors should treat them respectfully and cautiously. As seen on Discovery Channel, Shark Week, Animal Planet, and many more shows.

Relaxing on the Beach and Getting up Close to Wildlife

Compass Cay has several beautiful beaches perfect for sunbathing, relaxing, and activities such as kayaking. One of the most popular beaches is Rachel's Bubble Bath, a unique natural pool only accessible during low tide. During high tide, bubbles fill the Bubble Bath and it's a great spot for taking Instagram-worthy photos.

Compass Cay is also home to various wildlife besides sharks, such as sea turtles and iguanas. The wildlife is very accustomed to human visitors and you can often see them up close in their natural habitat.

Getting Involved in Local Activities and Tours

Several activities and tours on Compass Cay allow you to experience the island to its fullest. Fishing charters, scuba diving, snorkeling boat trips, and kayaking are all popular choices.

Accommodations:

Accommodations on Compass Cay are inviting and in tune with their natural surroundings. All individual villas are nestled among native vegetation, affording the utmost in privacy and beauty. All homes offer spectacular views of the marina, Pipe Cay, and the Exuma Sound. Accommodations are equipped with everything you need for an enjoyable stay. Full kitchen, bath, and linens included for both short and long-term stays.

Compass Cay in the Exuma Cays is a destination, offering visitors the chance to experience the best of the Bahamas in stunning and unique surroundings. Whether you want to interact with nurse sharks, relax on the beach, or get involved in the local culture, there's something for everyone on Compass Cay. So why not plan your next adventure to Compass Cay today?

Contact Compass Cay

Marina Reservation ONLY

+1 (242) 422-7300 Bahamas—Marina Reservations

Email: Reservations@Compasscaymarina.com or tucker11645@gmail.com

Housing Reservations ONLY

PLEASE USE the email below for Rental Information and reservations.

Email: captweemo1951@gmail.com

The phone is +1 (772) 532-4793 and will only be answered when in the USA.

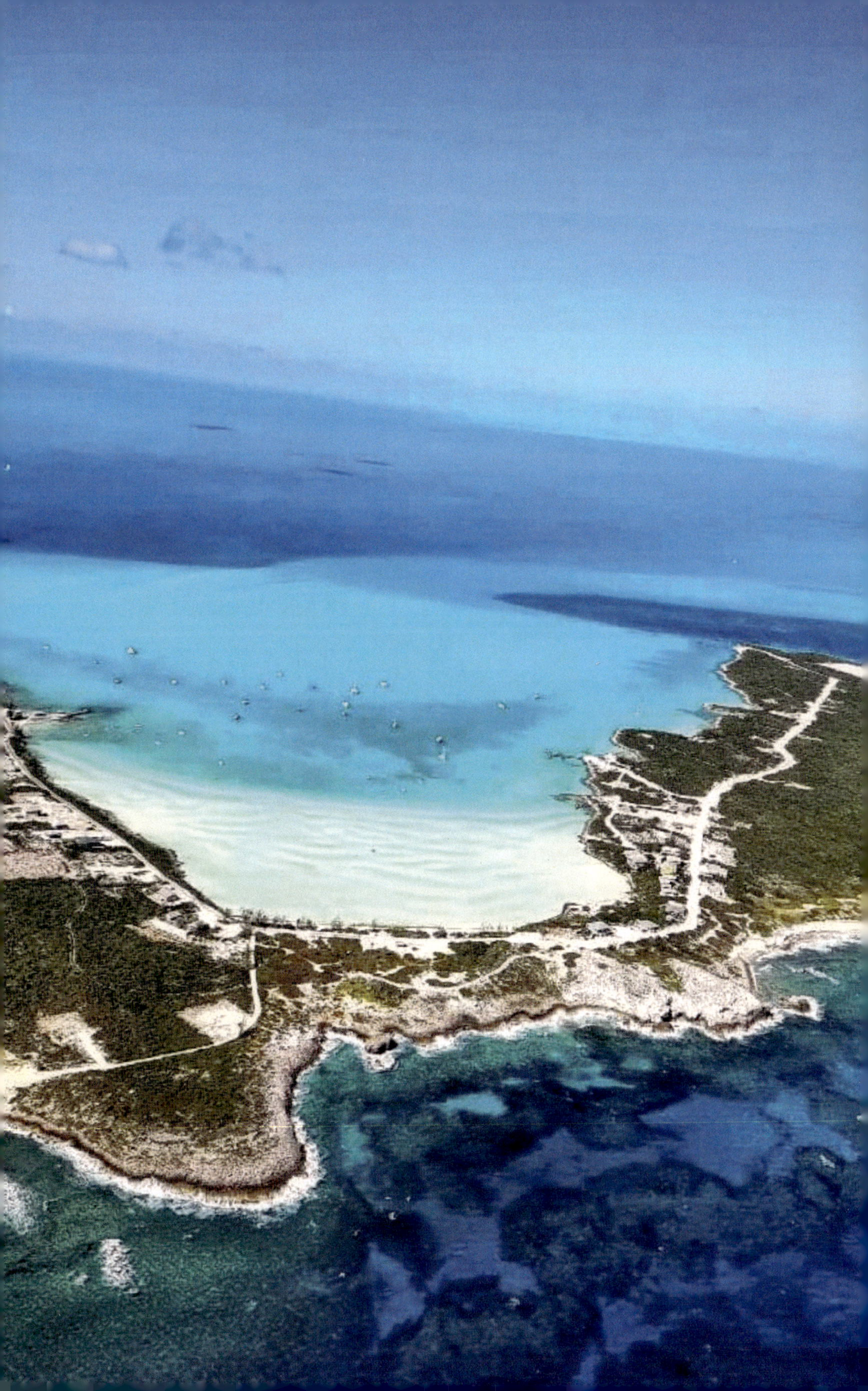

CHAPTER *Thirteen*

FLAVORS OF THE BAHAMAS: A CULINARY JOURNEY THROUGH AUTHENTIC BAHAMIAN RECIPES

Discover the Essence of Bahamian Culture with Iconic Cocktails

Every trip to the Bahamas isn't complete until you're sipping on a Bahamas Mama or indulging in a Bahamian Rum Punch. These iconic cocktails are not just drinks, they're a delicious blend of the islands' rich history and vibrant culture. And, of course, you must try a James Bond Martini while sitting in the Staniel Cay Yacht Club.

These cocktails are not just beverages, they're a portal to the Bahamas' rich cultural tapestry. Having a Bahama Mama or a Bahamian Rum Punch is a tradition when visiting the island, and every bartender knows how to make them.

Whether you're a travel enthusiast looking to immerse yourself in local traditions or a cocktail lover eager to explore new flavors, these beverages offer a taste of paradise you will want to experience. Cheers to new adventures and unforgettable flavors! 🌴🍹

The Bahama Mama

The Bahama Mama has captured the hearts of many, and its origins add a layer of intrigue to its taste. Oswald Greenslade, a renowned Bahamian bartender and mixologist, claims to have created this delightful concoction. Greenslade, who worked at the Nassau Beach Hotel in the 1960s, penned *One More Cocktail: A Guide to Making Bahamian Cocktails.* This book features astounding cocktail recipes, including the well-loved Bahama Mama and other creative drinks like the Splish Splash and Bikini Below the Knees.

Although Greenslade began working and crafting cocktails at the Nassau Beach Hotel in 1961, the Bahama Mama was already a famous cocktail in the 1950s. That suggests that Greenslade's recipe may have been a unique twist on a beloved drink, further enhancing its flavors and popularity.

Bahamian Rum Punch

Equally enticing is the Bahamian Rum Punch, a staple that perfectly encapsulates the spirit of the Bahamas. With its blend of tropical juices and local rum, the cocktail offers a taste of the islands in every sip. Whether lounging on a sun-soaked beach or enjoying a vibrant night out, a Bahamian Rum Punch is the perfect companion.

Ready to Explore More?

Dive deeper into Bahamian culture by trying these iconic drinks and discovering the stories behind them. Your Bahamian adventure awaits, one sip at a time!

Bahamian Rum Punch

The Bahamian Rum Punch is a staple drink that perfectly encapsulates the spirit of the Bahamas. With its blend of tropical juices and local rum, this cocktail offers a taste of the islands in every sip. Whether lounging on a sun-soaked beach or enjoying a vibrant night out, a Bahamian Rum Punch is the perfect companion.

Ingredients

- 1 1/4 ounces light rum
- 1 1/4 ounces dark rum
- 2 ounces pineapple juice
- 1 ounce orange juice, freshly squeezed
- 3/4 ounce lime juice, freshly squeezed
- 1/2 ounce grenadine

Top with maraschino cherry

Mix

1. Add light rum, dark rum, pineapple, orange, lime juices, and grenadine into a shaker with ice and shake until well-chilled.
2. Strain into a tall Hurricane glass over fresh ice.
3. Garnish with a maraschino or brandy cherry.

Note: The hurricane glass was modeled after the classic hurricane lamp—an oil lamp with a tall, protective glass chimney that shielded its flame from strong winds.

Vesper Martini Recipe

The Vesper Martini gained fame from its appearance in Ian Fleming's *Casino Royale* (1953), forever linking it to the suave James Bond. This cocktail, named after the enigmatic Vesper Lynd, is a captivating blend of simplicity and allure.

Ingredients

- 3 ounces gin
- 1 ounce vodka
- 0.5 ounces Lillet Blanc or dry vermouth
- Lemon peel (for garnish)

Mix

1. In a cocktail shaker, combine:

- 3 ounces gin
- 1 ounce vodka

- 1/2 ounce Lillet Blanc or dry vermouth
- **Optional:** For a classic touch, replace Lillet Blanc with Cocchi Americano to restore the original bitter flavor profile reminiscent of the Kina Lillet from James Bond's era.

2. Add ice to the cocktail shaker and shake vigorously until the mixture is well chilled.

3. Strain the mixture into a chilled martini glass.

4. Finish by garnishing with a twist of lemon peel on top.

5. Savor this timeless favorite immediately. Cheers!

Optional: For an added layer of complexity, incorporate bitters. Add three dashes of bitters to the Lillet Blanc before mixing. This will elevate the flavor profile, making it more reminiscent of the original recipe.

Lift your drink and toast to the enduring legacy of a classic cocktail. Here's to you and to unleashing your inner secret agent. Cheers!

Recipe for Gully Wash

Ingredients

- 1 ounces London gin
- 1/2 ounce sweetened condensed milk
- 2 ounces coconut water

Mix

1. Combine the gin, sweetened condensed milk, and coconut water in a shaker filled with ice cubes. Shake vigorously until the mixture becomes frothy.
2. Pour the mixture into a coconut shell or a fancy cocktail glass. Garnish with a drop of Angostura bitters on top of the froth for an extra kick of flavor.

Optional: For a fun Bahamian-style presentation, consider serving the Gully Wash in a coconut shell or an old-fashioned milk container. Gully Wash also gets better with time. Make it ahead (up to a week) and keep it chilled in the fridge. Remember to mix it thoroughly before serving.

How to Open a Fresh Coconut

Essential Supplies

- Corkscrew
- Hammer

Step-by-Step Guide

1. Make a hole in the "eyes."

- Locate the three spots on the coconut that look like finger holes in a bowling ball—these are the "eyes."
- Position the coconut with the eyes facing you.
- Insert the corkscrew into one of the eyes and twist until it goes through the meat inside.
- Repeat for another eye.

2. Remove the coconut water.

- Turn the coconut upside down and drain the water into a container.
- Sieve the coconut water to remove any fragments.

3. Crack open the coconut.

- Find the seam that runs between the coconut's eyes.
- Hold the coconut in your hand and gently tap along the seam with a hammer.
- Rotate the coconut while tapping until a crack forms.
- Continue tapping until the coconut splits into two.

Using Fresh Coconut Flesh

Fresh coconut flesh is versatile and flavorful. Here are some ways to use it:

- **Raw Snack:** Enjoy the sweet and nutty flavor of fresh coconut meat.
- **Cocktail Garnish:** Add an exotic touch to your drinks.
- **Coconut Milk:** Blend the coconut meat with water for a creamy homemade alternative.
- **Coconut Chips:** Bake slices of coconut for a crispy snack.
- **Shredded Coconut:** Shred and dry the meat for later use in various dishes.

Don't forget to share your Gully Wash with friends and family. Enjoy tropical cocktails together under the palm trees! 🥥🏝️

Introduction to *Flavors of the Bahamas: A Culinary Journey Through Authentic Bahamian Recipes*

Welcome to the vibrant world of Bahamian cuisine! *Flavors of the Bahamas* celebrates the rich culinary traditions passed down through generations. Each recipe tells a story of love, tradition, and the diverse flavors that make Bahamian food an unforgettable experience.

Discover the Rich Flavors of Bahamian Food

Bahamian food is more than just sustenance; it's a culinary adventure capturing the islands' hearts and souls. *Flavors of the Bahamas* features a collection of recipes I have learned from some of the best local cooks across the Bahamas carefully curated for you. From the pristine shores of Staniel Cay, Exuma Cays, Spanish Wells, and Ragged Island to charming Guana Cay Abaco, this cookbook is your passport to the islands' most treasured culinary secrets.

A Compilation of Culinary Wisdom

The recipes in this book aren't just instructions; they're a compilation of culinary wisdom and heritage. You'll discover the secrets of flavorful Bahamian dishes from exceptional cooks like Christine Linsley, Wade Nixon, Tyrone Cooper, Christine Sands, Jonnie, and Buda Pinder. Each recipe is a testament to the culinary diversity and richness of the Bahamas, offering you a chance to bring the authentic taste of the islands to your kitchen.

For Food Enthusiasts and Culinary Travelers

Whether you're a seasoned chef, home cook, food enthusiast, or culinary traveler, *Flavors of the Bahamas* inspires and delights. The recipes will remind you of your travels to the Exuma Cays and serve as your gateway to the vibrant world of Bahamian food. Through this book, you'll experience the diversity and richness of Bahamian cuisine and bring a piece of the Bahamas back to your kitchen.

Join Our Culinary Adventure

Ready to start cooking? Whether you're a traveler reminiscing about your time in the Bahamas or a local eager to explore your culinary roots, this cookbook is your guide to mastering Bahamian cuisine.

Grab your apron, gather your ingredients, and let's get cooking!

About Bahamian Cuisine

Bahamian cooking is a delightful blend of African, European, and Caribbean influences. Their use of fresh, locally sourced ingredients is a main component. The vibrant flavors will transport you to the Bahamas's sandy beaches and crystal-clear waters with every bite.

Key Ingredients in Bahamian Cooking

To truly appreciate Bahamian cuisine, it's essential to understand the key ingredients that give it its unique flavor.

- **Bird peppers.** These tiny, white-petaled flowers produce fruit beloved by birds and pack a fiery punch despite their small size. The birds share the bird pepper plants across the islands, often popping up in unexpected places.
- **Goat peppers.** Known for its deliciously sweet flavor and heat, like the habanero, this pepper is a local favorite. Its pods resemble mini pumpkins, changing from dark green to a peachy orange as they ripen.
- **Bananas.** Often grown locally, bananas add a sweet and tropical twist to many dishes.
- **Pineapples.** The Gregory Town pineapple claims to be the sweetest on the planet, and many state the Bahamas was the first country to produce pineapples commercially.
- **Guava.** Almost every area in the Bahamas can grow guava.
- **Mangos.** Grown in backyards across the islands, both savory and sweet recipes use mangoes.
- *Soursop.* High in vitamin C and locally grown. Some believe it's a cancer prevention.
- **Coconuts.** Bahamian cooking uses coconut water and meat extensively, providing a creamy and refreshing element to many dishes.
- **Thyme.** This herb is a staple in Bahamian kitchens, adding depth and aroma to various recipes. Many locals grow it in their yards.
- **Sea salt.** Harvested from salt ponds in the Bahamas, sea salt enhances the ingredients' natural flavors. Most kitchens keep it in a jar by the mortar and pedestal on their counters.

- **Lobster and crab "fat."** These seafood delicacies are central to many Bahamian recipes, offering rich and savory flavors. The "fat/butter"—also known as the tomalley, lobster paste, and crab fat—is a gooey mass inside the lobster's body that is part of its digestive system. YUMMY!
- **Yellow grits.** A traditional side dish, restaurants often serve yellow grits with seafood and stews.
- **Lime.** Known for its bright and zesty flavor, lime balances and elevates the taste of many dishes.
- **Old sour.** A mixture of lime juice and bird peppers many recipes include, but it works particularly well when seasoning fish and chicken. We keep a bottle of this in the refrigerator all the time. Some local stores even sell this as a premade mixture.

Bahamian Spiny Lobster

Bahamian lobsters, commonly known as spiny lobsters, belong to a family of over forty-five species of achelata crustaceans. Found in the pristine tropical waters of the Bahamas, locals harvest these lobsters (Panulirus argus) from August 1st to March 31st.

Bahamian lobsters, typically residing in the crevices of rocks and coral reefs, occasionally venture out at night to hunt for snails, clams, crabs, and sea urchins. They also take part in mass migrations across the sea floor, forming long lines that can include over fifty individuals.

The Bahamian lobster relies on its ability to detect the smell and taste of natural substances in the water, which vary across different ocean regions. They maintain group cohesion through physical contact, using their long antennae to stay connected. When threatened, Bahamian lobsters produce a loud screech by rubbing their antennae against a smooth part of their exoskeleton, deterring potential predators. These lobsters are social, often found in groups.

APPETIZERS

Mango by the Sea Summer Rolls

This delightful and tropical appetizer combines mango and fresh vegetables. It's reminiscent of a summer day in the Bahamas, eating mangoes in the sea. Perfect for parties, these summer rolls will make your vegetarian and vegan friends feel at home.

Ingredients

- 1 large ripe mango, peeled and sliced
- 1 medium jalapeño pepper
- 1/8 cup cilantro leaves
- 1 medium carrot, peeled and julienned
- 1/4 cup thinly sliced red onions
- 1/2 of a fresh lemon squeezed
- 1 small piece of ginger root (about 1/2 inch)
- 6–8 dry spring roll wraps
- 1/4 cup shoyu, tamari, or regular soy sauce
- 1/4 cup water
- 2 tablespoons chopped peanuts (optional)

Preparation

1. Prepare the vegetables

- **Peppers**: Cut the top off the jalapeño pepper and slice 3–4 of them small rounds, then place them in a dipping bowl. Julienne the rest for the rolls.
- **Ginger**: Cut a half-inch piece and grate it over a small bowl to catch the juices, then squeeze the juice from the grated ginger into the dipping bowl with the pepper rounds. Julienne the rest of the ginger for the rolls.
- **Carrot**: Peel and julienne the carrot.

2. Make the dipping sauce

- Add the soy sauce to the dipping bowl with the peppers, lemon, and ginger juice and stir well. Add water to dilute to taste. For a spicier dipping sauce, add red pepper flakes.

3. Assemble the rolls

1. **Prepare your work area**: Place 1 cup of water on a large, shallow backing sheet.
2. **Rehydrate the rice paper wrappers**: Drop each rice paper wrapper in the water and make certain the water covers it for about 5 to 10 seconds. You will feel it soften. Carefully remove it from the water, letting any excess drip off, and place it on your clean work surface.
3. **Add the filling**: Position your filling ingredients in the lower third of the wrapper.
4. **Fold and seal**: Fold the bottom edge of the rice wrapper over the filling and roll it forward one complete turn to cover the filling. Softly apply downward pressure on each end of the wrapper to seal the ends, then fold each side toward the center. Continue rolling forward until the entire roll is sealed.

5. **Serve**: Place the completed rolls on a serving platter, and make sure they do not touch so they do not stick together.

Tips: If the filling is slightly loose, don't worry; the rice paper will stick to itself, and additional sealing is unnecessary.

Experiment with different fillings such as bell peppers, cucumbers, or green onions for variety.

Before serving, sprinkle chopped peanuts over the finished rolls for added crunch and flavor.

This quick and easy recipe takes approximately fifteen minutes of prep. Enjoy your refreshing Mango by the Sea Summer Rolls with the delicious soy ginger dipping sauce!

Staniel Cay's Island Salsa

Ingredients

- 1 small pineapple, chopped
- 1 large mango, chopped
- 1/2 goat (scotch bonnet) pepper, finely chopped (adjust to taste)
- 1/2 red onion, chopped
- 1/4 cup cilantro, finely chopped
- 1/4 cup cucumber, chopped
- 1/4 cup red onion, chopped
- 1/4 cup red bell pepper, chopped
- 2 teaspoon salt
- 1/4 cup fresh lime juice (or to taste)

Preparation

1. Prepare the ingredients:
- Chop the pineapple and mango into small, bite-sized pieces. Then, finely chop the scotch bonnet pepper, red onion, cilantro, cucumber, and red bell pepper.

2. Mix the ingredients:
- Combine the pineapple, mango, scotch bonnet pepper, red onion, cilantro, cucumber, and red bell pepper in a large mixing bowl and add salt to taste. Squeeze fresh lime juice over the mixture, ensuring all components are coated well.

3. Chill:
- Cover the salsa and chill in the refrigerator for at least 30 minutes before serving. This allows the flavors to meld together beautifully.

4. Serve:
- Serve with cassava chips.

Serving suggestions: This vibrant, zesty Staniel Cay Salsa is perfect for any party or gathering. Its sweet and spicy flavors, paired with the crunch of fresh ingredients, will transport your taste buds to paradise. Enjoy!

Spanish Wells Stuffed Crab

Take a culinary trip to Spanish Wells with this delightful crab appetizer that's sure to be a hit at any gathering. Inspired by fond memories of visits to Spanish Wells, this recipe brings the rich flavors of fresh crab, buttery breadcrumbs, and aromatic herbs to your kitchen.

Ingredients

- 6 giant whole white crabs (Phillips Jumbo Crab Meat, in a can, be used as an alternative)
- 3 cups breadcrumbs (fresh breadcrumbs made from a loaf of Bahamian Bread or store-bought whole loaves)
- 3 tablespoons butter or margarine
- 1 medium onion, finely chopped
- 1 medium green pepper, finely chopped
- 1 tablespoon thyme
- Salt to taste

Preparation

1. Boil the crabs.

- Wash the crabs thoroughly. Then, place them in a medium pot and add about 1 inch of water to cover the bottom of the pot. Boil the crabs for 30 minutes over medium heat.

- Remove the crabs from the pot and let them sit until they are cool enough to handle. You can rinse them under cold water to speed up the cooling process. Some people wear latex gloves to protect themselves from the heat of the shells.

2. Prepare the crab meat.

- Remove the apron. The "apron" on a crab is a triangle of shell on the bottom of the crab (smaller and narrower on males, more prominent and broader on females). Remove it by grabbing the point toward the front of the crab and pulling it off.
- Remove the carapace. After removing the apron, you will see a small hole between the body and the top shell at the back of the crab. Hold the body with one hand and pull off the top shell by grabbing the shell where that tiny hole is. The liquid that comes out is called "crab fat," some people save it for use in soups or as a dipping sauce.
- Remove the gills and mandibles. Once the top of the shell is gone, the crab's digestive system becomes visible. Pull off and discard the two rows of opaque, feathery gills along the top. Snap off and discard the mandibles—two pointy things at the front of the crab. Rinse out the guts under cool running water. Then, pick the meat from the crab's claws, legs, and body and set the meat aside.

3. Create the stuffing.

- Melt the butter or margarine in a pan over medium heat and add the chopped onion and green pepper to the pan. Cook until lightly browned. Then, add the breadcrumbs, thyme, salt to taste and mix well. Finally, stir in the picked crab meat and crab fat. Combine thoroughly.

4. Stuff and bake.

- Preheat your oven to 400°F (200°C). While it's preheating, stuff the mixture into the crab back shells. Place the stuffed shells on a baking sheet and bake for approximately 15–20 minutes until golden brown.

Serving tips: Serve hot and enjoy this taste of Spanish Wells! This recipe yields six delicious servings. **Bon appétit!**

Whether you're reminiscing about trips to Spanish Wells or trying this dish for the first time, this crab delight will become a favorite!

Bahama Conch Bites with Goombay and Spiced Rum Dipping Sauces

Ingredients
- Conch Bites

- 4 medium conchs (I keep a frozen 5 pound box from the Bahamas Food Service in my freezer. Sysco in the States sells them)
- 2 eggs
- 1 cup flour
- 1/2 cup lime or lemon juice
- 1/2 cup evaporated milk
- 1 hot pepper
- 1/2 cup oil
- Traditional Bahamas Dipping Sauce
- 2 tablespoons ketchup
- 2 tablespoons lime juice
- 1 tablespoon mayonnaise
- 1 tablespoon hot sauce
- Salt and pepper to taste

Instructions

Conch Bits

1. Tenderize the conch.
- Use a meat tenderizer or mallet to pound (bruise) the conchs on both sides until they are tender. Be careful not to break the meat into pieces. Then, lay the tenderized conch flat in a pan and cover with salted boiling water. Remove the conch when the water has cooled. Pat dry with a towel.

2. Prepare the conch.
- Dice the hot pepper and mix it with the lime or lemon juice. Then, in a separate bowl, whip the eggs and evaporated milk together. Next, cut the conch into bite-sized pieces and allow them to sit in the lemon juice mixture for two minutes. Remove and shake off any excess liquid.

3. Coat the conch.
- Dip the conch pieces into the flour and shake off the excess. Next, dip them into the egg mixture, then back into the flour.

4. Cook the conch.
- Heat the oil in a pan over medium heat. Pan-fry the conch pieces until they are golden brown. Place the cooked conch bits on a platter lined with paper towels to absorb excess oil.

Goombay Dipping Sauce

1. Prepare the sauce.
- Dice and crush the garlic finely. Next, combine all the ingredients in a bowl. Mix until smooth. I always add a bird pepper, but you can add any hot sauce you like.

2. **Chill**: Pour the dipping sauce into a small bowl and chill before serving.

Spiced Rum Dipping Sauce

Ingredients

- 1/2 cup spiced rum
- 1/2 cup orange juice
- 1 tablespoon lemon juice
- 1 tablespoon lime juice
- 1 tablespoon sugar
- 4 tablespoons butter (optional but adds a rich flavor)

Preparation

1. Combine the spiced rum, orange juice, lemon juice, lime juice, and sugar in a saucepan.
2. Cook the mixture over high heat, stirring occasionally, until it reduces to a syrupy consistency.
3. Gradually add in butter, one tablespoon at a time, stirring continuously until the sauce thickens.
4. Keep the sauce warm until ready to serve.

Enjoy these delicious conch bits with the refreshing Goombay Dipping Sauce and delicious Spiced Rum Dipping Sauce. They will be a hit, so consider preparing a backup batch in your kitchen! For a different twist, you can also serve them with tartar sauce. Enjoy!

Bahamian Conch Fritters Recipe

Discover the authentic taste of the Bahamas with mouthwatering conch fritters paired perfectly with a zesty dipping sauce. This cherished Bahamian recipe brings a taste of the islands right to your kitchen. Conch, a prized shellfish known for its unique flavor, is often hard to find outside the Bahamas, making these fritters a true culinary treasure. Whether you're serving them as an appetizer, an irresistible finger food, or a delectable hors d'oeuvre alongside your favorite tropical drink, these fritters promise to be a hit. Experience a slice of paradise with every bite! Many claim Penny Nixon has the best conch fritter on Staniel Cay.

Ingredients

Fritters:

- 1 1/2 cups conch, ground or chopped fine (about 2 medium-sized conchs)
- 1 large hot pepper
- 1 medium onion
- 1/4 medium green bell pepper
- 1/4 red bell pepper
- 1/4 yellow bell pepper
- 2 stalks of celery chopped
- 3 cups flour
- 3 teaspoon baking powder
- 1 cup water or beer, I use a Kalik or Sands Bahamian
- 1 egg
- 1 tablespoon tomato paste
- 1 teaspoon chopped/smashed bird pepper or goat pepper to taste
- 1 tablespoon Thyme
- Salt to taste

Island Sauce:

- 1/2 cup ketchup
- 2 teaspoon mayonnaise
- 1 teaspoon hot sauce
- 1 teaspoon Worcestershire sauce

Optional: Or serve with Spiced Rum Dipping Sauce.

Preparation

1. Prepare the ingredients.

- Finely chop the onion, sweet peppers, and hot pepper. Then, run the conch through a food processor until finely chopped. Next, in a large bowl, combine the processed ingredients with flour, baking powder, water, egg, tomato paste, hot sauce, salt, and thyme. Mix well to form a batter.

2. Adjust the batter.

- The batter should be thick enough to drop from a spoon. If it's too runny, add more flour to thicken. Add a little water or beer to soften if it's too stiff.

3. Fry the fritters.

- Heat oil in a deep fryer or deep pot to 350F. Be cautious while handling hot oil! Next, drop the batter into the hot oil, using a tablespoon for large fritters or a teaspoon for small ones. Use a cooking fork to turn each fritter, ensuring they become golden brown on all sides. The conch fritters should float to the surface and be light and fluffy when done. Remove the fritters from the oil and place them on a pan lined with paper towels to drain excess oil.

4: Prepare the Island Sauce

- Blend ketchup, mayonnaise, hot sauce, and Worcestershire sauce until smooth. Chill the sauce and serve it on the side with the fritters.

Freezing and Reusing Batter: You can freeze any excess conch fritter batter for later use. When ready to use, remove it from the freezer and defrost it at room temperature before continuing. Once defrosted, add 2 teaspoons of baking powder and mix until well blended. Adjust the consistency with flour or water and add seasoning to taste. I often freeze small bags for use when we have an impromptu game night.

Enjoy your Bahamian Conch Fritters with the zesty Island Sauce for an authentic taste of the Bahamas Islands!

Bahamian Lobster Fritters Recipe

Ingredients

Lobster Fritters:
- 3–4 medium crawfish tails
- 1 medium onion, finely chopped
- 1 celery stalk, finely chopped
- 4 1/2 cups flour
- 2 cups water
- 3 tablespoons baking powder
- 2 hot peppers
- 2 tablespoons tomato paste
- Cooking oil for frying

Hot Pepper Sauce:
- 1 tablespoon oil
- 6 jalapeno peppers, minced again, I use bird pepper, or you can also use goat, but use only one
- 2 tablespoons ketchup
- 2 tablespoons vinegar
- Pinch of salt

Preparation

1. Prepare the crawfish tails.

- Boil the crawfish tails for 45 minutes. Allow them to cool before removing the meat from the shells. Then, cut the crawfish meat very finely.

2. Make the fritters.

- In a large bowl, combine the crawfish meat with the onion, celery, flour, water, baking powder, hot peppers, and tomato paste. Mix the ingredients until they form a thick batter.

3. Fry the fritters.

- Heat cooking oil in a medium-sized pot or deep fryer. Next, use a teaspoon to drop 1/2 teaspoon of the batter into the hot oil. Fry the fritters until golden brown.

4. Prepare the Hot Pepper Sauce.

- Mince the hot peppers. Then, mix the oil, minced peppers, ketchup, vinegar, and a pinch of salt until smooth.

5. Serve.

- Serve the fritters hot with the freshly made hot pepper sauce on the side for dipping.

  Enjoy your flavorful Bahamian Lobster Fritters!

To enhance the spicy and savory flavors of your Bahamian Lobster Fritters, consider these flavor-boosting tips:

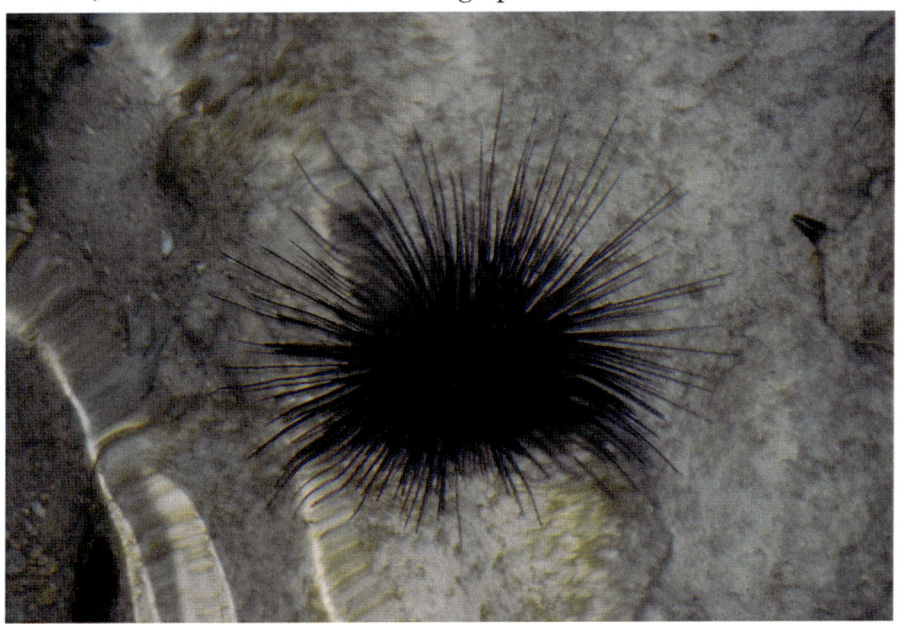

Flavor Enhancements:

Spicy Boost

- **Extra peppers.** For more heat, add a variety of hot peppers, like habanero or cayenne. You can also increase the number of peppers in the fritters and the sauce.

- **Chili powder.** Incorporate a teaspoon of chili powder into your batter for a smoky spice.
- **Pepper sauce variation.** Swap some ketchup for sriracha or another hot sauce to intensify the spicy kick.

Savory Depth

- **Garlic.** For extra depth, add 2–3 cloves of minced garlic to the fritter batter. This will enhance the dish's overall umami profile.
- **Herbs.** Integrate fresh herbs such as chopped cilantro or parsley to bring a refreshing contrast to the fritters.
- **Cheese.** Mix in a handful of grated sharp cheddar cheese or parmesan for a rich, savory note.

Additional Tips:

Seasoning. Ensure the mixture is well-seasoned with salt and a pinch of black pepper to balance flavors.

Marinade. For an added layer of flavor, marinate the crawfish tails in lime juice, garlic, and hot peppers before boiling.

These enhancements will amplify the existing flavors and create a more dynamic tasting experience. Enjoy your spicy and savory Bahamian Lobster Fritters!

SOUSES AND SAUCES

Discover the Flavors of the Bahamas With a Local Sunday Breakfast: Bahamian Boiled Fish

Imagine starting your day with the tantalizing aroma of freshly boiled fish wafting through the air. Sound intriguing? Welcome to a classic Bahamian breakfast experience—a feast for the senses perfect for breakfast and dinner! Bahamian Boiled Fish has been a staple in Bahamian cuisine for generations, reflecting the island's rich culinary history and its close relationship with the sea.

The Bahamas, a stunning archipelago of over seven hundred islands, cays, and rocky outcrops, is a seafood lover's paradise. But it's not just the abundance of seafood that makes Bahamian cuisine special. It's the skill and tradition behind the art of cooking, making it a staple for any meal.

The Art of Boiling Fish

Bahamians have mastered boiling fish, an art passed down through generations. Most prefer boiling meatier options like grouper or hog snapper because of their delicate, white, flaky texture and mild flavor that pairs perfectly with Bahamian spices.

When preparing this Bahamian delicacy, cooks cut the fish into large pieces or leave it whole, with the option of keeping the bone in or taking it out. Larger fish provide more succulent meat and have larger bones that are easier to remove while eating. Yet, a word of caution—always keep an eye out for hidden bones, even in fillets, as they can sometimes sneak through.

Why You Should Try It

For food enthusiasts and travelers alike, a local breakfast offers a unique taste of the Bahamas that's hard to resist. Whether strolling along a sandy beach or exploring the vibrant local markets, this dish is a must-try for those seeking authentic Caribbean flavors.

If you're not visiting this tropical paradise soon, indulge in this local favorite at home and savor the distinctive flavors of the islands in your own kitchen. Bon appétit!

Bahamas Boiled Fish Recipe

Experience the taste of paradise with this traditional Bahamian Boiled Fish recipe. Perfect for a Saturday morning breakfast or any time you crave a nutritious, high-protein meal. Serves 4–6.

Ingredients

- 2 pounds grouper or preferred fish (6 medium pieces)
- 1 medium onion, sliced
- 1 medium potato
- 2 hot bird peppers
- 2 limes and/or sour orange juice
- Water
- Salt to taste
- 1 bay leaf
- 1 teaspoon Thyme
- 4 whole allspice

Preparation

1. Prepare the fish.

- Thoroughly clean the fish and remove the scales and any blood remnants around the bones to ensure a clean broth. Place the cleaned fish in a bowl of ice water while you prepare the other ingredients.

2. Assemble the pot.

- Remove the fish from the ice water and place it in a 6- to 8-quart pot. Cover the fish with the sliced onions.

3. Add flavor.

- Crush one hot pepper and combine it with the lime or sour orange juice. Pour the mixture into the pot over the fish. Add the sliced potato, bay leaf, and enough water to cover the fish. Add a teaspoon of salt, increasing the amount to taste later.

4. Cook the fish
- Cook the mixture over medium heat until the fish and onions are tender, about 20 minutes. The broth should have a tangy, limey flavor, and the fish should be tender yet firm.

Serving Suggestions: Pair the boiled fish with traditional Bahamian sides of grits and Johnny cake with a slice of lime and a bird pepper for a truly authentic meal. Enjoy the taste of the Bahamas!

Experience the Delight of Bahamian Chicken Souse

Imagine waking up on a sunny Bahamian morning to the inviting aroma of chicken souse—a versatile dish that graces tables for breakfast, lunch, dinner, and even as a midnight snack. In the Bahamas, chicken souse is more than just a meal; it's a cherished tradition, a comforting bowl of goodness that brings families together and delights travelers seeking authentic island flavors.

In the Bahamas, Sunday mornings mean gathering around the breakfast table for a hearty serving of souse. Paired with steaming hot grits, fluffy Johnny cakes, or warm homemade rolls, it marks the weekend with joy and satisfaction. But the allure of chicken souse doesn't stop at breakfast. It's perfect for lunch to brighten your day or as a midnight indulgence that rejuvenates you after a vibrant night of dancing and revelry.

Some might think souse is just boiled chicken, but true culinary adventurers know the magic lies in its preparation. There's an art to crafting the perfect chicken souse—a delicate balance of flavors only skilled hands can achieve. Chris, our local souse maestro, can expertly transform simple ingredients into a masterpiece that warms the soul.

For those seeking new culinary experiences, visiting the Bahamas is not complete until you savor this beloved dish. Chicken souse invites you to explore the island's rich culture, one delicious bite at a time. Come, indulge in the taste of the Bahamas, and discover why chicken souse is a favorite among locals and travelers alike. Your adventure in flavor awaits!

Chicken Souse Recipe

Serves 6-8 people.

Ingredients

- 5 pounds of chicken wings cut up
- 1 medium onion, sliced thin
- 3 potatoes, peeled and cubed
- 1 stalk celery, chopped
- 1/2 cup lime juice
- 1 hot pepper, finely chopped
- Salt to taste
- 2 carrots, thinly sliced (optional)
- 1 bay leaf

Preparation

1. Prepare the chicken.

- Clean the chicken wings and drums with lime juice and water. Then trim them to remove as much fat as possible. Next, combine half of the lime juice with the hot pepper. Finally, wash the chicken with lime and salt water, then marinate it with ¼ cup of the lime juice and sprinkle with salt. Allow it to sit for 30 minutes.

2. Boil the chicken.

- Put a large 8- to 10-quart pot over medium heat, place the marinated chicken into the pot and cover with water. Bring to a boil, then remove from heat after 5 minutes. Discard the water to remove the oil extracted from the chicken skin, leaving the chicken in the pot.

3. Add vegetables and seasonings.

- Return the pot to the stove and cover the chicken with onions, potatoes, celery, and the remaining lemon juice mixture. Add water until it reaches about 1 inch above the contents, then season with salt. Add the bay leaf and optional carrots for extra flavor.

4. Simmer.

- Bring to a boil, then cover the pot. Reduce heat and allow to cook at medium-low heat for 1 hour or until the chicken and potatoes are cooked through. To avoid overcooking smaller potatoes, add them to the pot 30 minutes into the cooking process.

5. Adjust **the** seasoning.

   Taste and adjust seasoning if necessary.

   Serving Tips: Serve hot with grits, Johnny cake, bird pepper, and lime slices.

Bahamian Conch Chowder

Bahamian Conch Chowder is an iconic dish and a cherished part of Bahamian cuisine for generations. It showcases the island's bountiful marine resources and culinary traditions. From its succulent conch meat to aromatic spices, Bahamian Conch Chowder is more than just a meal—it's a flavorful testament to the Bahamian people's enduring heritage and culinary artistry.

Ingredients

- 4 cups finely chopped conch (some prefer to grind it)
- 1/4 cup cooking oil
- 1/4 pound salt pork diced small
- 1 tablespoon salt
- 1 medium onion, chopped
- 1 cup diced tomatoes (fresh or canned)
- 2 tablespoons tomato paste
- 1/2 teaspoon black pepper
- 4 quarts water
- 2 bay leaves
- 1/4 teaspoon allspice
- A bundle of fresh thyme tied with a string.
- 2 large carrots chopped
- 4 cups cubed potatoes
- 1 cup diced celery
- 1/2 cup finely chopped ham
- 1 cup Worcestershire sauce (Lea & Perrins preferred)
- 2 bird peppers
- One can of Campbell's alphabet soup (optional)

Preparation

1. Tenderize and prepare the conch into small pieces.

2. Prepare the base.

- In a large pot over medium heat, add 4 quarts of water. Then, add spices, carrots, potatoes, celery, and ham. Bring the mixture to a simmer.

3. Cook the salt pork.

- Add the cooking oil to a large frying pan over medium heat. Once hot, add the salt pork and cook until it turns light brown. Next, add the chopped onions and sauté until tender. Add the diced tomatoes and cook until they dissolve, then stir in the tomato paste and cook for an additional 5 minutes.

4. Combine and cook

- Transfer the contents from the frying pan to the large pot with the simmering vegetables. Add the conch and salt to taste. Bring everything to a boil and cook for 30–40 minutes, stirring occasionally.

5. Final Touches

- Add the Worcestershire sauce and bird peppers. Stir in a can of Campbell's alphabet soup (optional).

6. Rest and serve.

- Remove the pot from heat and allow the chowder to rest for 15 minutes before serving.

Get ready to savor the rich flavors of your hearty Bahamian Conch Chowder!

Stewed Conch Recipe

Stewed conch is a traditional Bahamian breakfast dish known for its rich flavors and tender texture. Often enjoyed with grits, Johnny Cake, Potato Bread, or homemade leaven bread, this dish brings a taste of the islands to your table.

Although sunny days are an everyday occurrence in the Islands of the Bahamas, we also enjoy occasional days when liquid sunshine falls to fill our cisterns. These rainy, sunshiny days, especially in summer, are when crabs come out and scurry around the island. We say, "The crabs are walking," and the crab pens fill. We feed the crabs white rice and vegetables for a few days to "Clean them out." Once done, the crab pots come out to enjoy a traditional Bahamian delight.

Ingredients

- 6 Conchs, cleaned
- 1/2 cup cooking oil
- 1 cup flour
- 1/2 teaspoon salt
- 1/2 teaspoon white pepper
- 1/2 teaspoon thyme
- 1 small onion, chopped
- 1 cup tomato, finely chopped
- 5 cups water

Preparation

1. Bruise the conch.

- Use a mallet or other object to tenderize the conch. If times are tough, you can always use an empty beer bottle. The goal is to break down the tough muscle fibers in the conch, making it more tender and easier to cook.

2. Boil the conch.

- Place the conch in a pot of water. The water should cover the conch. Boil the conch for 20–30 minutes. If you have thoroughly bruised the conch, it should be closer to 20 minutes. Don't worry, the wait will be worth it!

4. Make the stew base.

- Heat the cooking oil over medium-low heat in a large frying pan or medium-sized pot. Add the flour and salt to the oil, stirring constantly until the mixture turns golden brown.

5. Add the vegetables and seasonings.

- Add the chopped onion, white pepper, and thyme. Continue stirring until the onions become tender. Then, add the finely chopped tomatoes and cook until well blended with the other ingredients.

6. Combine and simmer
- Pour in the water and simmer the mixture for 10 minutes. If needed, add more water to thin it out. Add the boiled conchs to the mixture and cook for 30 minutes or until tender.

Serving Suggestions: Stewed conch is not just a dish, it's a tradition in Bahamian breakfast. Serve it with grits, Johnny Cake, potato bread, or homemade Bahamian bread for a delightful meal that will connect you to the rich culinary heritage of the Bahamas. Enjoy!

Spanish Wells Crawfish Bisque Recipe.

Here are some ways to take your bisque to the next level and make it even more irresistible!

Ingredients

- 1/4 cup of crawfish, finally chopped
- 1 quart of milk
- 1 piece of onion
- 2 pieces of celery, finely chopped
- 1 sprig of parsley
- 1 bay leaf
- 1/3 cup of butter, melted
- 1 1/2 teaspoons of salt.
- Pinch of pepper, about 1/8 of a teaspoon.

Preparation

1. Make the milk.

- In a pot on the stove, heat the milk with the onion, celery, parsley, and bay leaf to let the tasty flavors steep into the milk. After heating the mixture until warm, pour through a strainer to remove any solid particles and aside for later.

2. Prepare the roux.
- In another pot, combine the butter with the flour and a pinch of salt and white pepper to make a smooth roux. Mix over gentle heat continuously until the mixture takes on a slightly golden hue. Creating this roux will give your soup more flavor and richness. Gradually mix the flavored milk into the roux with a whisk and make sure there are no clumps while stirring over gentle heat until the mixture reaches the thickness you prefer.

3. Add the crawfish.
- Gently mix in the diced and cooked crawfish into the creamy soup until well blended.

4. Serve and enjoy.
- Serve the soup hot with croutons or toast sticks for a delightful dining experience. Savor the rich flavors with every spoonful you take.

Serving Suggestions:
- Add a bit of sherry or white wine to the mix. Adding some sherry or white wine, about two tablespoons, after you mix the milk and roux can bring out a slight sweetness that pairs well with the richness of the bisque.
- Add a hint of cayenne pepper. If you like a bit of spiciness, adding cayenne pepper can enhance the flavors of the dish while giving it a kick, without overshadowing the subtle taste of crawfish.
- Add some citrus. Adding grated lemon zest to the soup right before serving can enhance the taste by giving it a refreshing hint of citrus that balances out the creamy texture.
- Add fresh herbs. When cooking your bisque, you may default to using dried herbs; however, adding fresh herbs, such as dill, tarragon or chives, at the end not only enhances the flavor but also gives it a vibrant look, with a lovely garnish.
- Swap out the milk. Swap out half of the milk with a seafood broth to intensify the taste, further bringing out the rich seafood notes in the bisque and adding a touch of luxury to its flavor profile. Additionally, for a more indulgent bisque, substitute a portion of the milk with heavy cream. The increased fat will lend your soup a smooth texture and more intense flavor.

- Swap out the crawfish. Convert your crawfish bisque into a crab bisque by substituting the crawfish with cooked or flaked crabmeat and tweak the seasonings according to your preference! This adaptability lets you accommodate flavor choices and explore new culinary possibilities in your kitchen.

Adding these ingredients can elevate your traditional crawfish bisque into a gourmet delight that will amaze your loved ones and guests alike.

Salads

Bahamian Coleslaw

Bring a taste of the Bahamas to your table with this vibrant and soul-satisfying coleslaw. Inspired by the colorful Junkanoo Festival, this dish is a staple on many Bahamian tables. It's an easy way to add color and flavor to your meals. While no one can duplicate Milly's Coleslaw, I have tried repeatedly and this is as close as I could get.

Ingredients

- 1 small cabbage head, finely shredded
- 1/4 small red cabbage head, finely shredded
- 1 medium carrot, grated
- 1/2 sweet pepper
- 1 small onion, finely diced
- 1 bird pepper
- 1 teaspoon lime juice or more to taste
- 1/4 teaspoon sugar
- 1/8 teaspoon salt
- 2–3 tablespoons mayonnaise
- 1 apple, finely chopped (optional, for an extra festive touch)

Preparation

1. Prepare the vegetables.
- In a large bowl, combine the shredded green cabbage, red cabbage, sweet pepper, grated carrot, sweet pepper, and diced onion. Then, sprinkle the sugar, salt, bird pepper, and lime juice over the vegetable mixture. Next, add the mayonnaise and stir until all ingredients are well combined.

2. Chill.
- Refrigerate the coleslaw for at least 10 minutes to allow flavors to meld.

3. Serve.
- Just before serving, give the coleslaw a final mix. To add a little extra festivity, incorporate the finely chopped apple.

Serving Suggestion: Serve this Bahamian coleslaw with your favorite main courses as a refreshing side dish. It's perfect for barbecues, picnics or as a colorful addition to your everyday meals.

Enjoy the vibrant flavors and colors of the Bahamas in every bite!

Bahamian Conch Salad Recipe

When you visit the Bahamas, trying the authentic conch salad is a must! This dish perfectly blends the flavors of the islands using fresh and tangy ingredients that will surely delight your taste buds. You can also experiment with a tropical conch salad variation by replacing tomatoes with fruits for a unique twist on this traditional recipe.

Ingredients

- 2 medium-sized conch shells
- 1 onion, finely chopped
- 1/2 bell pepper, finely chopped
- 1 small tomato, diced (or swap with a tropical fruit like mango, pineapple, or apple)
- Juice of 3 limes
- Juice of 1 orange or 2 tablespoons freshly squeezed orange juice
- 1 bird pepper, finely chopped (adjust to taste)
- Salt, to taste

Preparation

1. Prepare the conch

- Rinse the cleaned conchs with a mix of lime juice and salt. Then cut into bite-sized chunks.

2. Mix the ingredients

- In a large bowl, mix the chopped conch with the onion, bell pepper, and tomato (or your chosen fruit). Then, squeeze the lime and orange juice over the mixture before adding the finely chopped bird pepper and a pinch of salt to taste.

3. Marinate

- Thoroughly blend all the ingredients and allow to sit and soak up the flavors for 10 minutes before serving.

Serving Suggestions: Indulge in the lively tastes of the Bahamas by savoring this conch salad. Customize it by swapping out tomatoes with your preferred fruit, such as apples, mangoes, or pineapples, to add a tropical touch to your mealtime enjoyment.

1. For added flavor and texture, try adding diced avocado or cucumber.
2. If you can't find fresh conch, you can also use frozen or canned conch.

3. To make the dish more filling, serve the conch salad on a bed of mixed greens or with a side of plantain chips.
4. For a spicy kick, add some hot sauce or extra bird pepper to your liking.
5. This dish is best enjoyed fresh, so aim to consume it immediately after preparing it.

Try out this Bahamian Conch Salad and enjoy the flavors of the islands! 🍹🥭🍍🦐

History of Conch

Conch has been integral to Bahamian cuisine and culture for centuries. The inhabitants of the Bahamas and other parts of the Caribbean have long relied on the bountiful marine creature surrounding their islands. Conch shells have been found in archaeological sites, and there is evidence of their use by indigenous populations, such as the Lucayan people, who were among the first inhabitants of the Bahamas. Traditionally, the conch was not only a vital source of protein but an important cultural symbol. Ancient peoples have used the shells as tools, musical instruments, and even in art and jewelry. Over time, conch has become synonymous with Bahamian cultural identity, celebrated in local festivals and enjoyed in various culinary forms, from delicious salads and chowders to beloved fritters. With its tender meat, this mollusk provides a taste of the ocean that continues to bring people together in an idyllic Caribbean backdrop.

Bahamian Crawfish (Lobster) Salad

Elevate your Bahamian Crawfish (Lobster) Salad with delicious and creative additions. Whether you want to add flavor, a bit of crunch, or a tropical twist, this salad is part of the way of life during crawfish season.

Ingredient Additions

1. **Fresh herbs such as c**ilantro or parsley. Add a handful of chopped fresh cilantro or parsley for a burst of freshness that complements the rich lobster meat.
2. **Fruits such as m**ango or pineapple. Diced mango or pineapple adds a sweet, tropical flavor that balances the savory and spicy elements of the salad.
3. **Vegetables.** Diced cucumber adds **a refreshing crunch and an additional layer of texture.** Finely chopped celery can provide a delightful crunch and a hint of earthiness.
4. **Spices.** A dash of smoked paprika can add a subtle smoky flavor **to** enhance the overall taste. Old Bay, a classic seafood spice blend, can bring out the natural flavors of the lobster.
5. **Dairy.** Replace half of the mayonnaise with Greek yogurt for a lighter, tangier dressing.

Preparation Enhancements

1. **Marination.** Pre-marinate the lobster by tossing the lobster chunks in a bit of lime juice and salt before mixing with other ingredients. This will allow the lobster to absorb more flavor.
2. **Presentation. One idea is to** serve the salad in avocado halves for a beautiful presentation and an extra creamy element. **You can also** bake small tortillas over an upside-down muffin tin until crispy to create edible bowls. Fill them with your lobster salad for a fun and crunchy serving option. **And many restaurants** serve the salad on chilled plates or bowls to keep it cool and refreshing.

Serving Suggestions

1. **On a bed of greens.** Combine mixed greens like arugula, spinach, and butter lettuce as a base for the salad. The greens add a nice contrast in texture and make the dish more substantial.
2. **In a sandwich.** Serve the salad in a toasted brioche roll for a luxurious lobster roll experience.
3. **With chips or bread.** Serve with crispy plants or warm pita bread for a delightful texture contrast.

Final Touches

1. Drizzle of olive oil. A drizzle of extra virgin olive oil can add a rich, fruity note to the salad.
2. Extra lime zest. Grate some lime zest over the salad just before serving for an extra pop of citrus flavor.
3. Microgreens. Top the salad with microgreens for a visually appealing and nutritious garnish.

History of Bahamian Crawfish (Lobster)

The Bahamian crawfish, Panulirus argus, holds a rich history deeply intertwined with the culture and cuisine of the Bahamas. Often called the spiny lobster, this delicacy has been a staple in Bahamian diets for centuries due to the abundance of the creatures. Fishing for crawfish in the Bahamas is not just a means of sustenance, but a significant cultural and economic activity. Locals eagerly anticipate crawfish season, typically August to March, and it marks a time when families and communities come together to celebrate and enjoy the seafood delight. Preparation methods have evolved and African, European, and Caribbean culinary traditions have influenced them, leading to the diverse dishes we see today. Bahamian crawfish salad is a standout favorite.

Enhanced Bahamian Tuna Salad Recipe

Ingredients

- 2 cans of tuna (in water) or fresh steamed tuna
- 1 lemon/lime
- 1 tablespoon mayonnaise
- 1/2 hot pepper
- Salt and pepper to taste

Additional Ingredients for Enhanced Flavor

- 1 tablespoon Dijon mustard
- 1 small red onion, finely chopped
- 1 celery stalk, finely diced
- 1 small bell pepper, finely diced
- 2 tablespoons chopped fresh parsley
- 1 teaspoon capers (optional)
- 1 teaspoon sweet relish (optional)

Preparation

1. Prepare the tuna.

- Open the tins of tuna and drain the water. If using fresh steamed tuna, flake it with a fork. Next, add the tuna into a medium bowl and mince with a fork.

2. Mix the ingredients.

- Squeeze the juice of the lemon or lime into the bowl. Add the mayonnaise, Dijon mustard, finely chopped red onion, diced celery, diced bell pepper, chopped parsley, and capers (if using). Next, finely chop the hot pepper and add it to the bowl. Sprinkle salt and pepper to taste.

3. Combine well:

- Mix all the ingredients thoroughly until well combined. Chill in the refrigerator for at least 30 minutes to allow the flavors to meld together.

Serving Suggestions: Bahamian Tuna Salad is incredibly versatile and can be served in many ways:

- For breakfast, pair it with creamy grits for a hearty start to your day.
- For lunch, serve it on Johnny cake or freshly baked bread, place it on a bed of crisp lettuce for a light and refreshing salad, or stuff it into a pita pocket or a tortilla wrap for a quick, on-the-go meal.
- For dinner, use it as a filling for stuffed tomatoes or bell peppers for a nutritious and visually appealing option.

Note: Feel free to get creative with this recipe—add your favorite ingredients or try different serving styles to make it your own!

This enhanced Bahamian Tuna Salad is a delightful blend of flavors and textures. Whether you're enjoying it for breakfast, lunch, or dinner, it will become a favorite in your meal rotation. Bon appétit!

The History of the Bahamian Tuna Salad

The Bahamian Tuna Salad has roots deeply entrenched in the culinary traditions of the Bahamas. The use of canned and fresh tuna became popular among Bahamians due to the abundance of fish and its accessibility in the region. Over time, Bahamians paired this versatile ingredient with locally available produce, such as lime and hot peppers, to create a dish that embodies the island's vibrant flavors. Initially a simple dish, the tuna salad evolved as local cooks experimented with additional ingredients and spices, enhancing its taste and making it a staple in Bahamian households. Whether enjoyed with a singalong by fishers or served at local gatherings, the salad has become a beloved dish that reflects the fusion of native and introduced influences in Bahamian cuisine.

Rice and Pasta Dishes

Bahamian Crab 'N' Rice

Ingredients:

- 3–4 medium Bahamian land crabs (legs and claws included)
- 4 ounces salt pork, ham, or bacon drippings
- 1/4 cup cooking oil
- 1 teaspoon browning
- 1 small onion, chopped
- 1 celery stick, chopped
- 2–3 sprigs of thyme
- 1 1/2 tablespoons tomato paste
- 3 cups long grain rice
- Salt and pepper to taste

Optional Additions: To elevate the flavor and add more depth to this traditional dish, consider incorporating the following ingredients:

Vegetables:

1 bell pepper, chopped—adds a touch of sweetness and color.

2 cloves garlic, minced—for a more aromatic and rich flavor.

1 carrot, grated—a subtle sweetness and texture.

Spices and Herbs:

1 teaspoon paprika—for an added layer of smoky flavor.

1 bay leaf—enhances the overall aroma and taste.

1 teaspoon crushed red pepper flakes—for a bit of heat (optional).

Liquids:

1 cup coconut milk—substitute for some of water to add a creamy texture and tropical flavor.

1 cup chicken broth—Replace some of the water for a richer taste.

Preparation:

1. Prepare the crab.
- Separate the crab's back from the body using a knife. Next, remove the brown substance ("crab fat") from the interior and secure it in a bowl. Avoid bursting the bitter gall bag (a small sac usually hidden under the fat). Then discard the apron, gills, gall, and back shell (unless you plan on stuffing the crabs later). Finally, clean the crab body, cutting it into 2–4 pieces depending on size. Slightly crack the claws and set aside.

2. Prepare the broth.
- In a large pot over high heat, add cooking oil and salt pork/ham fat/bacon. Cook until crispy, stirring occasionally. Then, add onion, celery, bell pepper, carrot, garlic, and thyme. Cook until the onions are tender. Finally, add crab fat, tomato paste, browning, paprika, red pepper flakes, bay leaf, and a teaspoon of salt. Stir vigorously and allow to brown for 2 minutes.

3. Cook the crab.
- Add the prepared crab pieces and continue mixing, letting it cook for another minute. Then add 2 cups of water and 1 cup of coconut milk (or chicken broth). Bring to a boil.

4. Cook the rice.
- Add the rice, ensuring the liquid level is 1 inch above the rice. Stir to distribute the rice throughout the pot evenly. Bring to a boil uncovered until the water evaporates from the surface. Turn the rice 2–3 times, rotating from the bottom of the pot to the top. Cover, lower heat, and allow to cook for 25–30 minutes or until the rice is fluffy and fully cooked.

Chef's Tips:
- Taste as you go to adjust the seasoning as needed.
- For extra richness, you can add a small knob of butter before serving.
- Garnish with fresh herbs like parsley or cilantro for added freshness.

Enjoy your enhanced Bahamian Crab 'N' Rice, packed with bold flavors and traditional comfort!

History of Bahamian Crab 'N' Rice

Bahamian Crab 'N' Rice's roots are deeply embedded in the cultural and culinary traditions of the Bahamas. This dish evolved as a staple among the islands due to the readily available land crabs and the adaptability of rice in Caribbean cooking. Traditionally, Bahamian cuisine reflects a blend of African, European, and indigenous influences, and Crab 'N' Rice showcases this fusion through its bold flavors and comforting appeal. The technique of cooking rice with seasonings and protein traces back to West African cooking methods brought to the Caribbean during the Transatlantic Slave Trade. Over time, locals incorporated their own ingredients and flavors, resulting in a dish symbolizing resilience and resourcefulness. Today, it remains a beloved component of Bahamian gatherings and celebrations, highlighting the nation's diverse heritage and the communal joy of sharing a flavorful meal.

Bahamian Macaroni 'N' Cheese Recipe

One piece is never enough. Even during school lunch breaks, this macaroni and cheese brought in lucrative revenues for a budding entrepreneur! A staple side dish to a Bahamian meal, macaroni and cheese is also a regular accompaniment for Sunday dinners and Christmas feasts.

Ingredients

- 1 eight-ounce package of cut macaroni pasta
- 1 medium onion, chopped small

- 1/2 medium green bell pepper chopped small
- 1/2 medium red bell pepper chopped small
- 2 1/2 cups of sharp cheddar cheese, grated
- 1 tablespoon of butter or margarine
- 1 can of evaporated milk
- 2 eggs
- 1 medium hot pepper
- Salt and pepper to taste
- Dash of paprika (optional)

Preparation

1. Cook the macaroni:
- Boil macaroni in salted water until soft and slightly overcooked. Then, drain the water.

2. Mix ingredients:
- While the macaroni is still hot, add 1 1/2 cups of grated cheddar cheese, chopped onion, green bell pepper, butter, evaporated milk, eggs, hot pepper, thyme, salt, and pepper. Mix everything until well blended.

3. Prepare to bake:
- Pour the mixture into a well-greased baking pan. Sprinkle the remaining cheddar cheese on top and add a dash of paprika if desired.

4. Bake:
- Preheat your oven to 300F. Bake the macaroni and cheese for 30 minutes or until firm.

5. Serve:
- Remove from the oven and allow to stand for 15 minutes before cutting into squares and serving.

6. Storage:
- Allow any uneaten portions to cool at room temperature before storing in the refrigerator.

    Optional: Add a variety of cheeses or 1 teaspoon of thyme

Enjoy your Bahamian Macaroni 'N' and cheese, a dish that's bound to be a hit at any meal!

History of Mac and Cheese

Macaroni and cheese, or "mac and cheese," though widely recognized across various cultures, has become a beloved comfort food in the Bahamas, intertwining with the culinary traditions of the islands. The origins of

Bahamian mac and cheese trace back to its introduction by American and European immigrants, who brought cooking techniques of incorporating pasta and cheese. Over time, Bahamians infused the dish with their own flavors and ingredients, such as hot peppers and thyme, reflecting Caribbean cuisine's vibrant and spicy nature. This fusion resulted in a distinct Bahamian variant of mac and cheese, making it a staple at family gatherings, celebrations, and even entrepreneurial ventures, serving as a delicious emblem of cultural adaptation and innovation.

Meat Dishes

Bahamian Fire Engine Recipe

Origins of the Dish

Legend has it that Bahamian cooks add so much bird or goat pepper to this dish that it feels like your mouth is on fire and you'd require the emergency assistance of a fire brigade to quench the flames.

Ingredients

- 1–2 tablespoons vegetable oil
- 1/2 diced onion
- 1/2 diced green pepper
- 1 can corned beef
- Juice of 1/2 a lime
- 1 teaspoon thyme
- 2 tablespoons tomato paste
- Bird or goat pepper, to taste
- Salt and pepper, to taste
- Rice or grits for serving

Preparation

1. Heat the oil

- Heat a medium saucepan over medium heat. Add vegetable oil and heat until it shimmers.

2. Cook the vegetables

- Add diced onion and green pepper to the saucepan. Fry until softened, about 5 minutes.

3. Add corned beef and seasonings

- Add the corned beef, thyme, and lime juice to the pan. Break up the corned beef as it cooks.

4. Cook the mixture.

- Allow the corned beef mixture to cook for about 3 minutes, or until the beef and vegetables begin to come together. Stir in the tomato paste and bird or goat pepper.

5. Adjust the consistency (optional).

- If you prefer a "looser" consistency, add a bit of water to the corned beef mixture.

6. Final seasoning.

- Let the mixture meld for another 1–2 minutes, then season with salt and pepper to taste.

7. Serve

- Serve the Bahamian Fire Engine warm with rice or grits.

Enjoy the spicy, flavorful kick of this traditional Bahamian dish!

Beach Party Steamed Fish Recipe

This delicious recipe offers a Bahamian twist on steamed fish. Perfect for a beach party or any gathering, it will have your guests coming back for more! On the islands, first, we go out handlining, catching the snappers, then we head to the beach and get the fire going!

Ingredients

- 3–4 whole fish like snapper or 4- to 6-ounce pieces of grouper
- Salt and black pepper
- 2 lemons
- 1 hot pepper
- 1/2 cup cooking oil
- 1 medium tomato, diced
- 1 medium onion, thinly sliced
- 1 teaspoon thyme
- Water
- 1/2 cup flour

Preparation

1. Prepare the fish.

- For whole fish, clean and remove excess scales. With a sharp knife, score the fish diagonally from head to tail on both sides.
- For all fish, squeeze lemon juice over the fish, both inside and out. Sprinkle with salt and black pepper on both sides. Chop the hot pepper and smear into the score marks and over the body. Allow to sit for about 10 minutes.

2. Cook the fish.

- Heat the cooking oil in a medium frying pan. Once the oil is hot, coat the fish with flour and fry until golden brown. Then remove the fish from pan and allow to rest.

3. Finish the dish.

- Pour off 3/4 of the oil from the pan, then add the onion and thyme to the pan and cook until the onions are tender. Next, add the diced tomatoes and allow to fry until thickened before adding 3 cups of water to the pan and bring to a boil. Return the fish to the pan, reduce the heat, and adjust the seasoning. Squeeze a bit of lemon juice into the pan. Allow to simmer for 5 minutes.

Serving Suggestions: Serve this delightful steamed fish over white rice, peas 'n' rice, or peas 'n' grits. Round out your meal with some macaroni and cheese, coleslaw, or plantains on the side. Enjoy to your heart's content!

Tradition of Beach Party Steamed Fish

Beach parties have long been a cherished tradition in the Bahamas, bringing people together to celebrate, relax, and enjoy the islands' natural beauty. Central to these gatherings is cooking fresh seafood, with steamed fish taking center stage. Traditionally, Bahamians set up makeshift kitchens on the sands, using basic equipment and fresh ingredients from the ocean. The process of steaming fish at a beach party is as much about the communal experience as it is about the flavors. It's a time for families and friends to connect, share stories, and dance to the rhythmic beats of island music, all while surrounded by the soothing sound of waves crashing against the shore. The simplicity and freshness of the dish reflect the resourceful and vibrant spirit of Bahamian culture, making it a timeless favorite for generations, both past and present.

Bahamian Minced Crawfish Recipe

This Bahamian minced crawfish dish is a favorite in my family. The first time I had it, I was at Penny Nixon's house, and I thought I'd died and gone to heaven. After a plate of this, you will feel the same way. Bahamian home-cooked meals are indeed a delight.

Ingredients

- 2 large crawfish
- 1 medium onion
- 1 medium green pepper
- 1/2 teaspoon thyme

- 1 tablespoon tomato paste, diced
- 1 hot pepper
- Salt and pepper to taste
- 1 clove garlic, diced
- 1/4 cup cooking oil
- Water
- 1 teaspoon lime juice
- If you have it, lobster fat is the secret ingredient that makes the dish! Fry it up lightly before adding it to the crawfish.

Preparation

1. Prepare the crawfish.

- Remove the legs and "feelers" (claws are on New England lobsters) from the crawfish. Next, place the whole crawfish, legs, and feelers into a large pot with enough water to cover the bottom (about 1 1/2").

2. Cook the crawfish

- Cover the crawfish with a damp towel, cover the pot with a lid, and cook over medium heat for 30 minutes. When done, remove the pot from heat and allow to sit for 25 minutes before opening the lid and removing the towel. Next, split the crawfish and remove all the meat from the shell, including the head, legs, and feelers. Don't forget the "fat" from the head. Cut the meat into chunks and then shred or mince.

3. Cook the crawfish and vegetables.

- In a large frying pan over medium heat, add cooking oil. Once the oils it hot, add the crawfish, onions, green pepper, garlic, and thyme. Sauté until the vegetables are tender and the crawfish is slightly browned. Then, add the tomatoes, tomato paste, salt, and hot pepper. Cook for 5 minutes, stirring continuously. Add a dash of water, reduce heat, and simmer for 10 minutes.

Serving Suggestions: Serve the minced crawfish over white rice. Complement the dish with coleslaw and plantain on the side for a complete Bahamian meal experience. Enjoy your Bahamian minced crawfish!

Cooking Tips and Variants

- **Freshness matters.** For the best flavor, use fresh crawfish. You can use frozen crawfish, but the taste won't be as vibrant.
- **Balancing spice.** Adjust the amount of hot pepper based on your spice tolerance. If cooking for a crowd, consider using a milder pepper or providing spicy condiments on the side.
- **Herb enhancements.** Add a sprinkle of fresh cilantro or parsley at the end of cooking to give the dish a fresh, herby note.

- **Texture tips.** When mincing the crawfish, consider your preferred texture. Finely mincing produces a smoother dish, while larger chunks provide more bite.
- **Customization options.** Experiment by adding other vegetables, such as bell peppers of different colors or even corn kernels, for a sweet touch.
- **Citrus twist.** Add a splash of lime juice instead of lemon for a different citrus flavor that pairs well with seafood.
- **Serve with variety.** Though traditionally served with rice, this dish also pairs well with boiled potatoes or as a stuffing for bell peppers for a unique presentation.

History of Bahamian Minced Crawfish

The traditional minced crawfish recipe has a deep-rooted connection to the culinary culture of the Bahamas. Crawfish, or "Bahamian lobsters," thrive in the warm, clear waters surrounding the islands, making it a popular ingredient in local cuisine. The dish originates from the resourcefulness of Bahamian fishers, who used whole crawfish to create nourishing and flavorful meals for their communities. As they passed the recipe down through generations, each family added its touch, contributing to today's variations. Minced crawfish has found its place not only as a beloved family dish but also as a staple at local Bahamian restaurants, showcasing the rich culinary heritage of the islands.

Steamed Conch Recipe

Steamed conch is a delightful dish often prepared beachside, offering the freshest taste straight from the ocean. Here's how to make it:

Ingredients

- 2 fresh conch, cleaned
- 1 medium yellow onion, chopped
- 1 stick celery, chopped
- 2 cups of water
- 1 teaspoon green bell pepper, chopped
- 1 teaspoon dried thyme
- 1/2 teaspoon salt
- 1/2 teaspoon ground black pepper
- 2 tablespoons oil or butter (I use both)
- 2 fresh ripe tomatoes, skinned and chopped
- Juice of one lime

Preparation

1. Tenderize the conch.

- Tenderize the conch by bruising it with a meat tenderizer mallet. This helps soften the meat. Next, boil the conch for 10 minutes in just enough water to cover it, along with some butter, skimming off any foam. (Save the conch stock for seafood chowder or fish soup.)

2. Prepare the sauce.
- In a pan, heat the oil and/or butter and sauté the onions until they become translucent. Next, add the chopped tomatoes, green bell pepper, celery, and thyme to the pan. Pour in a little water and simmer gently until everything reduces into a thick sauce.

3. Cook the conch.
- Add the boiled conch to the sauce and simmer for an additional 5–10 minutes. Remove the foam from the water and season with salt and ground black pepper to taste.

4. Steam the Conch
- Place the conch in a tinfoil bag and add the chopped onions, celery, green bell pepper, tomatoes, herbs, and spices, along with some oil or butter and a bit of water to steam.

5. Serve
- Serve the steamed conch hot, paired with mac 'n' cheese and coleslaw for a complete meal that brings the beachside party to your dining table.

Serving Suggestion: For a richer flavor, you can also add a squeeze of lime juice over the conch just before serving.

Enjoy your delicious and freshly prepared steamed conch!

Steamed Conch

Steamed conch has roots deep within the culinary traditions of the Caribbean, particularly in regions where conch is abundant in the surrounding waters. Historically, conch has been a valuable source of protein for coastal communities, with its use in cooking dating back centuries. Scholars believe native Caribbean tribes first harvested and consumed conch meat, incorporating it into their diets long before European colonization. Over time, the preparation and enjoyment of conch have evolved, blending indigenous methods with influences brought by African, European, and Asian cultures. Today, steamed conch stands as a testament to a rich culinary heritage, celebrated not only for its delicious taste but also as a representation of the diverse cultural landscapes of the Caribbean nations.

Deserts

Rum Cake Recipe

Ingredients

<u>Cake Ingredients</u>

- 1 cup chopped pecans or walnuts (optional)
- 1 box (15 ounces) yellow cake mix
- 1 box (3 3/4 ounces) vanilla instant pudding and pie filling
- 4 eggs
- 1/2 cup cold water
- 1/2 cup vegetable oil
- 1/2 cup dark rum

<u>Glaze Ingredients</u>

- 1/4 pound butter
- 1/4 cup water
- 1 cup granulated sugar
- 1/2 cup Dark Rum
- Powdered sugar to dust the cake (optional)

Preparation

1. Prepare the Bundt pan.

- Preheat the oven to 325F. Thoroughly grease a standard-sized bundt pan with butter. You may also apply cooking spray if desired. Next, dust the inside of the pan with about 1 teaspoon of flour. Shake to distribute evenly. Sprinkle the nuts on the bottom of the pan.

2. Make the cake.

- In a mixer bowl, combine the cake mix, vanilla instant pudding, eggs, cold water, vegetable oil, and dark rum. Beat on medium until everything is well incorporated. Gently pour the batter into the prepared Bundt pan, trying not to disturb the layer of nuts. Bake for 45–55 minutes, or until the cake is golden brown, pulling slightly from the edges of the pan, and a toothpick inserted into the cake comes out clean.

3. Make the glaze.

- When the cake is almost finished baking, melt the butter in a small saucepan. Stir in the water and granulated sugar until the sugar dissolves. Bring the mixture to a boil and boil, stirring constantly, for 5 minutes. Remove the pan from heat and stir in the rum. Be cautious, as the mixture will spatter and froth up.

4. Finish the cake.

- Once the cake is done baking, immediately and gently run a thin knife around the outside edges and the center of the cake to release. Using a toothpick or wooden skewer, poke numerous holes into the cake. Then, spoon the glaze over the hot cake while it is still in the Bundt pan. Do this in 3 or 4 stages, allowing the glaze to absorb into the cake. Wait about 5 minutes between each stage.

- After using the last of the glaze, allow the cake to sit for 5 minutes. Turn the cake over onto a large cake plate or cake stand. The cake should slide out of the Bundt pan and onto the plate. Allow the cake to cool fully.

NOTE: The cake's flavor improves over time. Allow it to sit overnight, or at least six hours before serving. Enjoy!

While this rum cake offers a delightful mix of flavors and a rich, moist texture, it cannot compare to Jackie Sand's renowned rum cake. Jackie, a resident of Guana Cay Abaco, is famous for her extraordinary baking, which she employs to create an unrivaled rum cake. Her version is not just a dessert but a sensational experience, combining traditional methods with a secret ingredient that captures the essence of the island's rich culture and flavors. Though this rum cake is delicious in its own right, Jackie's creation has become a beloved staple for locals and visitors alike, garnering acclaim for its unmatched taste and perfect balance of rum and sweetness.

Made in the USA
Columbia, SC
07 February 2025

6698fe7a-2494-492e-840a-9e0867d7e5f1R02